On Becoming
Who We Are

On Becoming

Who We Are

Passionate Musings
in the Winter of Life

Barbara Fiand

A Crossroad Book
The Crossroad Publishing Company
New York

THE CROSSROAD PUBLISHING COMPANY

www.crossroadpublishing.com

Printed in 2013

©2012 by Sister Barbara Fiand

Crossroad, Herder & Herder, and the crossed C logo/colophon are registered trademarks of The Crossroad Publishing Company

In continuation of our 200-year tradition of independent publishing, The Crossroad Publishing Company proudly offers a variety of books with strong, original voices and diverse perspectives. The viewpoints expressed in our books are not necessarily those of The Crossroad Publishing Company, any of its imprints or of its employees. No claims are made or responsibility assumed for any health or other benefits.

The text of this book is set in Utopia.
The display font is Americana

Library of Congress Catalog information is on file.
ISBN 13: 978-0-8245-0024-5
Library of Congress Control Number: 2013932607

Books published by The Crossroad Publishing Company may be purchased at special quantity discount rates for classes and institutional use. For information, please email info@CrossroadPublishing.com.

In grateful memory of
Leon Lajoie, S.J.,
for what he taught me about integrity,
and
my mother,
for what she taught me about God

Thanks to the human heart by which we live,
Thanks to its tenderness, its joys, and fears,
To me the meanest flower that blows can give
Thoughts that do often lie too deep for tears.

—William Wordsworth
Ode: Intimations of Immortality from
Recollections of Early Childhood

CONTENTS

PREFACE

In a recent gathering of Catholic men and women the conversation drifted, as it frequently does these days, to issues involving our church and the seeming disunity so many of us feel. Disappointment and discouragement were voiced with the way regulations tend to come from ecclesial leadership without apparent consultation or even simple dialogue. The question then was raised why any one of us would not simply leave the church, abandon Catholicism, and become a nondenominational Christian. The answer that I found most fascinating came from a woman sitting across from me who simply said she could no more leave her church than she could change her gender, her race, or her blood type. "Catholicism is in my DNA," she said, "It is who I am."

It appeared to me that there was some kind of "Aha" experience in the group when she said this. We agreed that our religion is more important than the latest regulation or episcopal letter; that it is much bigger and broader than that, and cannot simply be identified with the chancery or the Vatican. We also noted that since the Second Vatican Council there had been a decisive emancipation among the laity in the church that had brought about this realization. Theology schools in the last forty plus years have had large numbers of lay women and lay men, Catholic sisters and brothers among them, earn advanced degrees, and the influx of laity in church ministries wherever it is permitted has been considerable. With education, being well read and informed, comes the increased ability to think, form one's conscience, and express one's views. The image of shepherd and docile flock no longer fits the model of church many adults are looking for and are trying to help build. Being asked to "submit one's intellect and will" to the views of the episcopate, regardless of, or in contradiction to, one's own formed conscience, simply implies to many adults that they are being asked to lie. The notion of obedience has moved from the medieval "divine right of kings" model, or the military "command/obey" model, to that of an informed democracy where discernment includes everyone, or at least a *representative* group.

The thoughts and reflections offered in this book are meant for the "DNA" Catholics I have described above. The topics covered in these "Musings" have been with me for many years and have evolved with me until finally my thinking, reading, searching, praying, and ageing have moved me into a place where the writer in me needed to respond. The connection between the four parts of this book came in the process of writing them. When I started to write, all I knew was that there were certain urgent concerns that needed yet to be thought through, put on paper in some orderly fashion, and offered to the reader for reflection. In part 1 of the book (chapters 1 and 2) I offer my explanation as to the why of this. It is a more personal disclosure than I am generally in the habit of making, but because of the time in my life and the climate of our times, I found it fitting.

Theology and spirituality are ultimately about our quest for God. As I have grown older, this quest has intensified, and at times I feel some impatience with what appear to me petty concerns and superficial, bureaucratic details that seem to keep us as church from this questing. For me this means they keep us from the big concerns of community, table fellowship, inclusion, love, and justice, which were the primary concerns of Jesus and should now be ours as his Body. If this impatience shows through in my writings, I beg the reader's indulgence. I find, as I get older, that this life is too short for pettiness and superficiality, and so I invite the reader to join with me and take courage: first, in freeing ourselves from the unnecessary burdens we need to let go of (chapters 3, 4, 5, and part of chapter 6), and then secondly (chapter 6 in part and chapters 7, 8, 9, 10) to plunge deep into the Mystery that defies all clear explanations and final resolutions, but is the ever alluring: *mysterium tremendum.*

My sincere thanks go once again to my friends and community for many stimulating conversations, but more than that for their patience in allowing me the space, time, and necessary solitude that the discipline of writing requires. A sincere thank you also to Springbank

Ecumenical Retreat Center for generously offering and providing me with time to think and write. As always a believer in the communion of saints and keenly aware of the many loved ones who have already passed on but are nevertheless present with us in our quest for global transformation, I want to thank them for their *felt* encouragement throughout my writing. I remember especially my dearest friend Clare Gebhardt S.N.D.; my parents, Wilhelm and Eisabeth Fiand; my faithful mentor and friend Leon Lajoie S.J.; for inspiration: Sebastian Moore O.S.B., Ron Terrence Colloty O.S.F., Pierre Teilhard de Chardin S.J.; for encouragement and love: Louise Stuhlmueller S.N.D., and Dorothy Stang S.N.D. Without your nudging, I may not have had the energy or courage to write. My thanks go also to my publisher for the kind support and encouragement and to the patient editors that worked with me so faithfully.

Part One

MUSINGS

Chapter 1
The Why of a Book
Such as This

Chapter 2
On Being a Pilgrim:
A Meditation

1

THE WHY OF A BOOK
SUCH AS THIS

It is our turn to learn what justification means
as Paul did long ago, not from books
but from the sights and sounds of God
in our lives.

—Regis Duffy, O.F.M.

Sometimes I think that I have been a teacher all my life. As a child in Germany I played school with my two sisters using (to my grandmother's dismay) the large shiny surface of our bedroom armoire as a blackboard. Later in high school I tutored, and immediately after graduating I taught sixth grade in a school on a Native Canadian reservation near Montreal when no licensed teacher could be found. With the exception of time out for studies and the occasional spiritual renewal period, I have been teaching ever since and have experienced every level of its lure from grade school to graduate school. Teaching has been my passion, almost my raison d'être. A profession undervalued and underpaid, teaching has been the love and pride of my life. Thomas More's admonition to Rich in *A Man for All Seasons,* "Be a teacher, Rich, be a teacher," sounded an echo deep within. "Be a teacher, Barbara, be a teacher," is what I hear in the depth of my heart even now, when I have formally retired from academic institutions and am beginning to "re-member" my life and to integrate my experience.

Being a woman in academe was never an attitudinally debilitating issue for me in the exercise of my call, even as I moved into the higher levels of teaching—so often still the realm of male dominance, especially in universities sponsored by religious orders of men or in seminaries, where I spent the majority of my graduate teaching years. It is clear to me now that I owe my position regarding my own gender to my mother—a tiny woman with extraordinary strength who singlehandedly weathered the storms of World War II (in the Asian theater of that tragic conflict) with three little daughters to care for and keep safe.[1] My mother was my security. They say that children's images of God frequently originate in their experience of their parents, and so it happened that with an absent father during the war years of my early childhood, my sense of the Divine approximated my experience of my mother, and the feminine was rooted in me. As a consequence, a sense of inferiority simply never infiltrated my conscious or even my subconscious mind. I knew men were allowed to do things in society that women were not, but that never drove me to the conclusion that, therefore, they were better or, for that matter, closer to God. Disappointment with, and anger at, the injustices of the official Catholic mentality toward women (when, through the years, I became aware of it) certainly altered my view of "catholicity"— so often ironically lauded as a "unity in diversity." It never, however, altered my conviction concerning both the fundamental equality of the genders and a woman's capacity to stand shoulder to shoulder with her male colleagues. To be sure, I suffered my share of what Walter Wink and others call the "domination system," but silently to accept the injustice done to me as a God-given or God-willed reality never occurred to me. I have, therefore, generally not been afraid to express my thoughts and to ask questions. The word "why" is and continues to be important to me.

As I grew and matured in the exercise of my teaching vocation, it became ever clearer to me that the primary task of the teacher is to provide time and to open up space for the emergence of the truth. This can be exhilarating in ideal circumstances, but quite often it is also an arduous and at times hazardous task, especially when one is involved with disciplines in which tradition has established what appear to be arbitrary standards of truth that cannot be violated. That the evolution of thought requires, of necessity, the adaptation of our understanding and of our subsequent view of reality seems to be a phenomenon surprisingly uncomfortable for many academics and is often feared, even hated, in the academy. I suspect that few if any disciplines are totally exempt here, but theology strikes me as particularly vulnerable. What surprised me when I first started to teach at a major seminary was the reticence with which evolving new ideas (and, therefore, in the Catholic "theater of thought" often identified as *controversial* topics) were being dealt with in the classroom.

The openness with which the faculty discussed these issues in the faculty dining room (especially in the beginning years of my tenure) was always refreshing and often very instructive for me. Classroom teaching, on the other hand, frequently seemed more like a political press conference. The "party line" was offered, and personal views were circumvented with such phrases as: "the teaching of the church on this matter is clear. . . ." It was rare that a professor stated respectful disagreement—giving personal research and thought, the perspective of prominent scholars, or even divergent views in the episcopate—and then invited student discussion.

The official stance against women's ordination, when it first became an "infallible pronouncement" by the last pope (made for him by the present pope) is a case in point. There had been a faculty decision to respond to questions regarding this matter by giving the official church teaching, and then, if appropriate, to cite divergent views from different Christian traditions, and, finally, respectfully to offer one's own perspective, *if asked.* In this particular case, the statement of "respectful disagreement but obedience" by the then archbishop of Milwaukee, Rembert Weakland, was mentioned as an example. Years of discussion around this topic had made it quite clear to me where most of us stood, but when I actually carried out our decision, I was alone, and this was most likely part of my "undoing." My eventual resignation from the faculty could not have come at a better time, however, both for my own intellectual integrity and my peace of mind, since now one is required to take oaths of (unquestioning) loyalty to the church's (or perhaps more accurately put, the Magisterium's) official position on all matters of faith and is expected, once again, to "submit one's intellect and will" to its utterances—even on topics such as Reiki, which, quite likely, are totally beyond its field of competence. It is clear that in such a climate Rembert Weakland's approach mentioned above would be unheard of.

Not long ago I came upon a book written by Sebastian Moore when he was very likely in his nineties. He had retired to his monastery after years of teaching in the United States. This, his last book, is entitled *The Contagion of Jesus: Doing Theology as If It Mattered.* I have read many of Sebastian Moore's works and I admire them greatly. In this book, however, more than ever before, I noted what seemed to me an unprecedented readiness to publish thoughts—homilies and essays—displaying a remarkable liberty of thought and creativity. They had been written over the years but had never previously been put to print. It occurred to me that retirement and being in the winter of one's life may have had something to do with this daring collection of thoughts. The aged were burned as witches or heretics in times past if they were suspected of straying from *the* path, but such abuse of power no longer is part of our religious practice today, thank God! What harm, really, can be done today to an ageing and retired theologian?

There is a certain freedom from domination that comes with retirement: seniors (even in the Catholic Church) may finally be able to say or write publicly what they have passionately thought for a long time (perhaps even for a lifetime) but most likely were never given the opportunity to voice openly. They may finally have the chance to be carefree and courageously to speak their truth. They may be able at last to redeem (free) themselves as teachers and scholars and to stir the embers of what may often appear as a dying fire. They may be able to do this—even if just a bit—to help liberate thought beyond the strictures of the academy into the evolving universe patiently waiting for us to "catch on."

This present book was inspired by what, rightly or wrongly, I intuited from my reading of Sebastian Moore's *The Contagion of Jesus,* as well as the books of John Dominic Crossan and Marcus Borg—some written in their retirement as well. They also speak of the "domination system," in both state and religious institutions, and of the reign of God that Jesus courageously proclaimed in opposition to it, and for which he died. While I was reflecting on what these scholars exemplified for me by speaking their truth openly, I happened quite synchronistically to come upon a 2007 book written by the well-respected French writer Olivier le Gendre, published in France by J. C. Lattès and titled: *Confessions d'un cardinal.* Le Gendre had been asked by a cardinal in Rome to interview him and write down his reflections on the church of today. The cardinal did not want his name mentioned. In his eighties and retired, he simply wanted to express in anonymity his concerns about the movement in our church as he saw it. He too models the freedom and the honesty that come with age—albeit in his case they are still somewhat restricted by where he lives.

There are a number of essays and lectures I have written in these past many years that have never made it into any of my previous books. There are also thoughts born of passionate musings that have fermented in my heart for years, thoughts that the teacher in me still wants to bring to the page. This book, at this time in my life (God willing), offers me that opportunity. It is not a closely structured and developed presentation working through one topic of particular concern, but rather a collection of thoughts (musings) sometimes overlapping and perhaps even at times repetitious for the sake of emphasis. The book may prove disturbing for some, exciting for others, or it may simply draw a "Yes!" from those who also have been thinking along the lines presented here and have been trying to contextualize their faith in a time-relevant manner.

As I have openly contended and frequently articulated, my research and involvement for most of the last thirty years of graduate teaching have been with the transformation of consciousness that is opening up for humanity during this time in history. We live in a period of radical change calling us toward realizations heretofore unheard of and unfathomed. The insights emerging in our day are demanding thoughtfulness and inner strength to let go of a paradigm that has held sway for several thousand years but is losing significance and power today.

I believe firmly that the revelations of our time are depending on us for articulation and conscious integration. Although they have been with us for a century or more and have already infiltrated our ways of seeing and thinking, albeit often unconsciously, they need to be formalized at this time in history; they need to be given the chance to enter into cultural and public awareness. On the religious and ethical front, these revelations offer us a paradigm to live by and pray in, a paradigm of transpersonal interconnectedness that will move us beyond fragmentation and toward global coordination and inclusiveness beyond creed, level of economic development, nationalism, and the endowment of natural resources. We are slowly being moved today to the existential realization that John Donne indeed was right: "No [one] is an island, entire of itself"; nor is any culture or economic structure isolated. "Every man [and woman] is a piece of the continent. . . . If a clod be washed away by the sea, Europe is the less, as well as if a promontory were [so also is America, and Asia, Africa, Australia, and Antarctica] . . . ; [anyone's] death diminishes me, because I am involved in [humankind]."

Like all paradigms before it, the paradigm presenting itself today with an ever greater urgency will not be a final and permanent model for understanding ourselves and our place in the world. It too will grow, develop, and change, as does the evolving human mind and heart where it finds its home. Today's model, however, is emerging *for us* and *in our time*. As such, it needs to be approached reverently and gratefully—for offering us today one further step into the Mystery that is our universe, pointing us to the divine unfolding *there*. Philosopher and systems theorist Ervin Laszlo assures us that

> our consciousness is not a permanent fixture: cultural anthropology testifies that it developed gradually in the course of millennia. In the thirty- or fifty-thousand-year history of modern man, the human body did not

change significantly, but human consciousness did. It
evolved from simpler beginnings and, if humankind
survives long enough, it will evolve further.[2]

Numerous great spiritual traditions have affirmed Laszlo's
view, as have contemporary philosophers and mystics from
Jean Gebser and Richard Bucke to Bernard Boelen, Beatrice
Bruteau, Ken Wilber, Chris Cowan, and Don Beck. Some of
them speak from personal experience, as does the mystic Richard Bucke, whom I have cited elsewhere.[3] Others speak from
the fields of philosophy, biology, cultural anthropology, and
social psychology. Pierre Teilhard de Chardin, a Jesuit paleontologist and mystic, was among the first and most prolific writers in our time to apply the theory of evolution to spirituality.
Much has happened in the past fifty or sixty years to support
him and to adapt our faith vision to the evolving consciousness of our time. This book, written in the winter of my own
life, is an attempt to continue and support this enterprise.

My meditations and musings on the Christian tradition— some short, others longer—are by no means meant to
be reactionary. They are, quite honestly and simply, my soul
questions into how and why I have come to recognize the
need for the articulation of my faith in a twenty-first-century
world-perspective. This present chapter, as well as the one that
follows, were written to make this clear. My hope in exposing, to some extent, my own journey is to highlight the path
that I, and many others like me, travel today in search of relevance and deeper meaning. This search, for those of us serious about our faith, is a life's task that involves serious study

and research, but also quite often a painful having to let go for the sake of faithfulness, a living in the void for some time, and a patient and humble waiting in the hope of "a better dawn." Above all, however, it involves claiming our responsibility as adult believers to ask the depth questions into God. It impels us to keep looking for and claiming the treasure—that Love that surpasses all understanding but desires, nevertheless, to speak to us in *our* time and *our* context in order to be meaningful in every age, not only to the learned few, but to all and for the sake of all.

2

ON BEING A PILGRIM: A MEDITATION

INTRODUCTION

At this time in history we are to take nothing personally. Least of all ourselves. For the moment that we do, our spiritual growth and journey comes to a halt. Gather yourselves. . . . All that we do now must be done in a sacred manner and celebration. We are the ones we have been waiting for.

—Message from the Hopi Elders,
Oraibi, Arizona Hopi Nation

Of late, spurred on by the questions of others, I have begun to reflect on my own pilgrim journey in greater detail. As strange as this may appear, it is not my habit to dwell on the specifics of my moving along my own spiritual path—on what I am doing, what spiritual practices I am engaged in. I sense somehow that I am involved with the Divine but often discover movement only in retrospect and with some surprise and puzzlement—not so much that it happened, but more, I suppose, *how* it did.

Some spiritual directors may find this approach questionable, but, then, I have not had many spiritual directors. I have done mostly private and silent retreats and have relied more on soulmates in my life, on those who are with me on a journey not clearly marked out, full of the unexpected; a journey of un-programmed wonder and awe in the face of life as a whole. I have admired Teresa of Avila, John of the Cross, and Ignatius, of course, but ever since the end of my novitiate days, I have resisted trying to figure out where I belonged in their scheme of things. A planned or programmed life has not seemed helpful to me and has, in fact, not worked out either. My dearest soulmate, Clare, one time told me that when she first met me, her impression was that I had simply stepped into her life and said, "Here I am, deal with me," and she did. Perhaps this is the attitude with which I have approached life in general and also God. And life as well as God does deal with me.

The question as to how the Spirit is working in the transformation of my understanding, of my conscious approach to my life and to the issues arising in this age of change is, nevertheless, a haunting one. My hope is that my struggle with it in this brief reflection may, at least, be one answer for those who are not attracted to specific "ways of perfection."

"How does transformation happen in me?" I wonder quite seriously whether at times or even generally, I tend to be somewhat of a "drifter," since, when it gets to my own spiritual life, it is rare that I set myself a task or make a resolution with a planned end point. In fact I have almost an abhorrence for "resolutions" and find "growth plans" burdensome. They appear too organized and controlling for me and, in the past, I have tended to ignore them almost immediately after I have formulated them. Nevertheless, the longing is in me; the hunger for the Deep pervades my every moment. It will not let me go. I keep searching.

BEING DRIVEN

For a long time, months, even years on end, I have tended to "read myself into" new ways of seeing. I am, as it were, driven to read, to acquire information, insights, wisdom; to see with the new worldview, to embrace history— finally revealed by daring souls with enough courage to identify old ways of seeing as inadequate and to explore the new. During this time of reading, my study does not consciously appear to me as necessarily intended or directed toward my own inner life. It looks more like the fulfillment of academic interests—for future courses, or writings, or just, and perhaps most importantly, to know and not to be kept in the dark any longer, no matter what the consequences. The feelings or emotions present in the spiritual arena of my life at that time often seem to be just neutral, quiet—as if nothing is happening. At most, there is simply excitement about daring ideas and accuracies regarding theories of science, history, exegesis, or women's issues, but my own personal journey is not the focal point. This neutral state can last a long time.

RECOGNITION AND WAITING

At some point, however, there comes a moment of recognition that my old ways of seeing no longer work for me; that they are over and that my life is in fact already quietly moving toward the new. The former ways of understanding seem almost gone. I know, of course, what they are, but sense that they are no longer relevant for me. After this insight, there often follows an emotional void in which I seem to drift. This void can be confusing and even somewhat painful at times, but it is not unbearable. It simply is. I continue to engage in old ways of worship, for example, but I feel and ponder this void. I am carried along in it, as it were, and my whole spiritual life appears to be floating or perhaps quietly gestating. I do not analyze this, nor do I analyze myself in it. Instead, I watch myself—something that feels like a "gazing" from beyond me. I may even write and teach during this time, and when I do, I feel the momentary "energy" of the new, but most often it feels tentative, not settled-in yet. There is little that I can do during this time to settle down on anything permanently, to "land the plane," as the saying goes, and there is no drive to do so. What is happening is beyond the systemic, beyond my formal intellectual training, beyond my will power, and to reflect on it rationally is useless.

EVENT

And then, all of a sudden—like birthing—there it is! What I have come to call "the Event" can come at any time. Sometimes it arrives as if "out of the blue." At other times, in a strange way, it happens "upon me" when I reread what I wrote months or years before and find myself fascinated with what I wrote, wondering where this came from. The Event is not necessarily grand. It does not have to be. It simply presents a kind of finality or closure, about certain things, ideas that have "ruminated" in the stillness. It can perhaps best be described as an "aha" experience mingled with a "Yes" to that closure, as well as to what is now emerging. There can be some sadness at what has to go, as well as some hesitation for a while to speak about it openly for fear of offending. There can also be loneliness and some impatience at the fact that what I have let go of is still being held on to by so many, and that the new is often maligned as inappropriate, out of place, lightweight, "New Age," as disrespectful of tradition.

I need to remind myself then of the differences in the human journey and how generalizations and declarations of certainty at any time are really a betrayal of the Spirit. There is, after all, no certainty or complete finality about anything at any time in the evolving and ever changing event of God's self-gift. All that is clear to me is that old certainties do not hold any longer; that they belonged to a particular moment in history, but that in an ever-evolving universe the new is constantly emerging and "presencing" in a process of ongoing and ever new revelation.

Recently a friend of mine shared with me copies of Margaret Wheeler Johnson's article in *Huffington Post* (December 29, 2011) titled: "Losing My Religion: If I'm So Done with Faith, Why Do I Still Feel Its Loss?" I read her comments with interest and in many respects felt solidarity with her views and her feeling of loss. I wondered, however, why I am not done with my faith. Her experiences and mine were the same: Catholic schools, catechism, exposition of the Blessed Sacrament, devotion to Mary, our teachers (mostly sisters demanding excellence), guilt (in huge quantities), confession, Sunday Mass. Both of us remember these experiences of our youth well. For her, however, they seem to have defined her religion, and, as an adult, years later, she no longer feels connected. She is done with them and the faith that inspired them. For me they are the past, one aspect of our religious tradition that needs contextualization in the evolution of thought. I do not reject them, but I have to admit that many of them no longer speak to me either. In *From Religion Back to Faith,* I tried to differentiate between those two aspects of any religious tradition. I see faith as deeper than religion as such and as instrumental in evolving religion beyond any particular cultural expression into ever new revelation. Perhaps my background in philosophy and hermeneutics and my study of scripture, exegetical research, and contemporary theology have helped me not to let go of the

Christian tradition, even as I bemoan the lack of leadership from the official "church" in reshaping the metaphysical formulations of the past and presenting them to a contemporary body of believers. There seems, instead, to be repetition upon repetition in the vane attempt to bring about insight for the believer desperately looking for relevance in our time. One can get exasperated with mindless reiterations of formulae and practices that no longer make sense, but (and here perhaps is our difference) if the longing is there, the search has to continue. As is so well said in the *Ecstatic Poems* of Kabir: "When the Guest is being searched for, it is the intensity of the longing for the Guest that does all the work. Look at me and you will see a slave of that intensity."

Faith is not something among other things. It is part of our transcendent human reality. It can be denied, of course, as Margaret Wheeler Johnson would seem to think. It can also be held on to mindlessly, as many others do, for want of anything better or out of guilt and fear. I believe that it needs to be struggled with, like Jacob struggled with the angel, and that eventually the dawn will break and with it, a new vision. I believe that for me there has to be a gentle "letting be" in the "letting go," rather than rejection on my part. "Releasement" is what the mystic Eckhart called it. It is necessary today, particularly because the *shift into the new* affects everything and, eventually and irrevocably, it will touch everyone. It is a recurring and universal aspect of human consciousness transformation that, as I mentioned already, actually is ongoing, though it is especially intense at this time of human history. It can occur on numerous levels: sometimes level by level, sometimes on all of them together and at once; but when it does, there generally is no turning back.

The words of William Blake, mystic and poet, seem particularly relevant here. In his prophetic book *Jerusalem*, he speaks most eloquently of the journey and of the wanderers we all are destined to be:

> *Trembling I sit day and night,*
> *my friends are astonish'd at me.*
> *Yet they forgive my wanderings,*
> *I rest not from my great task!*
> *To open the Eternal Worlds,*
> *to open the immortal Eyes*
> *Of [humankind] inwards*
> *into the Worlds of Thought:*
> *into Eternity*
> *Ever expanding in the Bosom of God,*
> *the Human Imagination.*
> *O Savior pour upon me thy Spirit of meekness & love:*
> *Annihilate the Selfhood in me, be thou all my life!*

The transformation of vision and the "wanderings" I go through (all seekers go through in various ways) are meant precisely to "open our immortal Eyes inwards into the Worlds of Thought: into Eternity ever expanding in the Bosom of God." For Blake, God and we are intertwined: "*I am in you and you in me, mutual in love divine.*" He has God say in an earlier part of this work: "*I am not a God afar off, I am a brother [sister] and friend; Within your bosoms I reside, and you reside in me: Lo! We are One; forgiving all Evil; Not seeking recompense!*"

Blake's vision concerning the divine-human interconnectedness of love is in many respects the vision that is emerging today out of what some call "quantum spirituality": spirituality's response to the discoveries of twentieth- and twenty-first-century science. As he prophesied in *Jerusalem*, however, it unfortunately was feared then, as it is also feared today. Nevertheless, it is ours to embrace, and the path is ours for the walking.

APPLICATION

What I have described here has happened in me at various times and most acutely during these latter years of my life. Most of the time it occurs quietly: A shift that does not eliminate yearning and questing for the More— even when there is insight and the temptation arises to "rest." The experience subordinates other experiences and convictions that I once may have held dear, though it does not necessarily always do away with them entirely. Somehow I am helpless in the face of this.

Right now, for example, "designated holy places" as such seem no longer enough for me. They have, of course, from time immemorial and almost universally been used by humankind to symbolize and remind us of the holiness that pervades the universe, cosmic sacredness.[4] As such they are indispensable today as much as ever, and I revere them. In the dualistic worldview that has pervaded most religions in modern times, we have, however, quite frequently separated the sacred and its symbols from life in general, and it is this dualism that I find no longer viable. Sacred rituals have in many respects become isolationist, the prerogative of the few anointed ones who bestow the sacred rather than helping us see its presence everywhere. This is particularly true today in my own religion where the insights of the liturgical reforms after the last Vatican Council seem progressively to be replaced by an intentional "sacred separatism" that highlights the boundaries of the holy rather than proclaiming its universal presence. As a consequence, I feel a deep need for a wider expanse: To return to the boundless beauty in nature and the sacred in ordinary people, to receive the "bread of life" there as well, and to recognize the Holy Presence, to let it touch me there, and to be suffused by it. My feelings of solidarity with Tom (Martin Sheen) in Emilio Estevez's film, *The Way* come to mind as I write this: He walks the Camino de Santiago ("The Way of St. James") in Spain. His purpose is to honor his son who was accidentally killed on this journey, to walk this road in memory of him, but also and primarily (even if unconsciously) to be healed himself. When he finally arrives at the shrine, his consolation and inner reconciliation come only as he leaves its overwhelming religiosity and grandeur and follows a trail to the ocean shore. There, in nature, together with his pilgrim companions, the brotherhood and sisterhood of seekers, Tom finally finds peace.

Peter Mayer, a modern poet and singer, also expresses well, and very simply, the shift I have been reflecting on here. In his music he sings of his gradual movement from restricted "sacramentality" and the emphasis on properly sanctioned sacred space and persons; from the denial or, at best, the forgetfulness of the holy in the everydayness of human existence to the recognition that *Everything Is Holy Now*, and the exultation that comes with this kind of conversion into depth.

> When I was a boy each week
> On Sunday we would go to church
> And pay attention to the priest
> He would read the holy word
> And consecrate the holy bread
> And everyone would kneel and bow
> Today the only difference is
> *Everything is holy now.* . . .
>
> When I was in Sunday school
> We would learn about the time
> Moses split the sea in two
> Jesus made the water wine
> And I remember feeling sad
> That miracles don't happen still

> But now I can't keep track
> *'Cause everything's a miracle. . . .*
> So the challenging thing becomes
> Not to look for miracles
> But finding where there isn't one
>
> When holy water was rare at best
> It barely wet my fingertips
> But now I have to hold my breath
> Like I'm swimming in a sea of it. . . .
>
> This morning outside I stood
> And saw a little red-winged bird
> Shining like a burning bush
> Singing like a scripture verse
> It made me want to bow my head
> I remember when church let out
> How things have changed since then
> *Everything is holy now.*[5]

God is indeed Holy Mystery, and all of us, from pope to pauper, are simply pilgrims—everyone poor and on the journey into the Divine. The miracle for our time in history, and a sign of transformation, is that teachers can be found and acknowledged today in the most unexpected places: often film producers and folk singers are speaking the vision now, and the lessons for today can be learned in many different venues. Revelation truly is ongoing, and God is indeed very good!

THOUGHTS AND QUESTIONS
FOR MEDITATION

1. "They say that children's images of God frequently originate in their experience of their parents, and so it happened that with an absent father during the war years of my early childhood, my sense of the Divine approximated my experience of my mother, and the feminine was rooted in me." Does this statement ring true for you? Is our God image parent-tied, and if so, how has this helped or hurt you in your spiritual journey?

2. Catholicity implies "unity in diversity." What is your reaction to this statement?

3. What do you understand by the observation that the evolution of thought requires, of necessity, the adaptation of our understanding and of our subsequent view of reality? Why would that be feared by academic or ecclesial establishments and considered as "controversial"?

4. "I believe firmly that the revelations of our time are depending on us for articulation and conscious integration. They need to be formalized at this time in history; they need to be given the chance to enter into cultural and public awareness. On the religious and ethical front, these revelations offer us a paradigm to live by and pray in, a paradigm of trans-

personal interconnectedness that will move us
beyond fragmentation toward global coordination,
and inclusiveness beyond creed, level of economic
development, nationalism, and the endowment of
natural resources." Are you ready for this task? This
book is intended to focus some of these issues.

5. "My hope in exposing, to some extent, my own journey is to highlight the path I, and many others like
me, travel today in search for relevance and deeper
meaning. This search, for those of us serious about
our faith, is a life's task that involves serious study
and research, but also quite often a painful having to let go for the sake of faithfulness, a living in
the void for some time, and a patient and humble
waiting in the hope of "a better dawn." Above all,
however, it involves claiming our responsibility as
adult believers to ask the depth questions into God.
It impels us to keep looking for and claiming the
treasure—that Love that surpasses all understanding but desires, nevertheless, to speak to us in *our*
time and *our* context." Can you relate to this hope?
Is it yours as well?

6. "As strange as this may appear, it is not my habit to
dwell on the specifics of my moving along on my
own spiritual path—on what I am doing, what spiritual practices I am engaged in. I sense somehow
that I am involved with the Divine but often discover movement only in retrospect and with some

surprise and puzzlement—not so much that it happened, but more, I suppose, how it did." Is this your experience, or do you prefer an ordered process of growth? What do you consider the most important aspect of the spiritual journey?

7. Have you experienced the quiet gestating dimension in your spiritual journey? Do you ever just gaze at what is happening in you or what you seem to be about? Can you do this without judging yourself or thinking something is wrong with you?

8. What have been the "aha" experiences of your spiritual life? Have they been joyful or at times filled with the anxiety or sadness of now having to let go of what seemed so certain at an earlier time?

9. "I believe that if the longing is there, the search has to continue. As is so well said in the *Ecstatic Poems* of Kabir: "When the Guest is being searched for, it is the intensity of the longing for the Guest that does all the work. Look at me and you will see a slave of that intensity." Are you that slave? Does your longing give you the energy to keep questing?

10. How has William Blake's "*I am in you and you in me, mutual in love divine.*" . . . "*Within your bosom I reside, and you reside in me: Lo! We are One; forgiving all Evil; Not seeking recompense,*" speak to you?

11. Can you relate to the movie *The Way*? Or to Peter Mayer's "Everything Is Holy Now"? If so, how?

Part Two

RATTLING THE IDOLS: REVERENCING THE HOLY

Chapter Three
The Question of Idols

Chapter Four
Because We Have
Never Done It

3

THE QUESTION OF IDOLS

To the third Christian Millennium is reserved the task of overcoming a tribal Christology which allows Christians to see the work of Christ everywhere without assuming that they have a better grasp or monopoly of the mystery, which has been revealed to them in a unique way.

—Raymond Panikkar

It would seem that idols and heretics have been in existence ever since humans began to organize their God relation and develop the notion that some ideas concerning the Mystery (usually their own) were better than others and needed to be recognized as such. This, one can surmise, eventually led to a claim of priority and to the persecution of those who disagreed. What for humans at first evoked an experience of awe in the face of transcendence and was wrapped in poetry, myth, and ritual, gradually, with the ascent of intellectual acumen, "morphed" into the dryer realm of theory and, as time moved on, into an entire system of belief. With increased cultural recognition and importance, the inviolability of this system was then declared and began to be seen as definitive truth revealed by the transcendent One "Himself"—either directly or through "His" chosen ones. From there it was only a short step before its adherents began to claim the right to subordinate, as well as to judge, all religious experience in terms of *their* doctrines and dogmas. Most "organized" religions, I suspect, and certainly the Christian denominations and sects, not only succumbed to this process, but were, in fact, its source, with some traditions suffering a greater systematization than others.

The dogmas and doctrines of many faith systems seem to make infidels and defectors inevitable. Historically, even in today's more liberated times, the "insiders" of religion (especially those who see themselves as the guardians and defenders of their own certitudes) understand disagreement as heretical, as pagan, as leading to idol worship, as relativism or secularism, and generally as outside the realm of the *truly holy*. They have tried and continue to try to convert dissenters, to persuade them, sometimes coerce them back into conformity with the system and, if unsuccessful, even to persecute them. Attempts at understanding and honoring diversity seem generally rare.

But what if the infidel and worshiper of idols is to be found not so much as the one who does not accept, or consider as important, some of the long-held religious truths of any particular faith system *but is, instead, the enforcer of the creed?* What if the Holy is denigrated by certitudes rather than honored and praised through them? What if definitive doctrines belittle the Mystery and stifle human questing, reducing the longing for the transcendent and inducing arrogance and self-righteous apathy instead? What if, therefore, the truly religious person of today sees the stringent and sometimes unexamined approach to dogmas and doctrines (often accompanied by excommunications and anathemas for the non–adherent) as ever less relevant in the face of the enormity, grandeur, and mystery of creation? What if she or he experiences this approach as in fact irreverent and arrogant and, as such, truly idolatrous?

The disagreements in our day between different religions and even sometimes *within* a particular faith system may certainly be disturbing and painful for those who consider themselves the guardians of the truth and see it as their "obligation" to persuade others to orthodoxy. Nevertheless, might not depth faith—*the honest search and longing for the "abyss of Mystery" and for the experience of silent reverence in the face of it*—be in today's world a much more authentic response to, and honoring of, the truly transcendent nature of the Holy One whom it sees as beyond all human definitions and certitudes? If these questions are on the mark, and numerous readings as well as conversations with other seekers (for me specifically within the Christian/Catholic Church) persuade me that very likely they are, it would perhaps be helpful to give some thought to where, in fact, the real danger lies. What is it, in other words, that *truly* threatens the fledgling movement in our time from certitude to authentic encounter and humble embrace of the eternal Mystery *as, indeed, Mystery*?

Not all of us have the endurance and courage necessary to accept the pain that this kind of questing entails and can easily fall prey to new idols that promise a reprieve in the longing and hunger for answers. But, what if the ecstasy is, in fact, primarily *in the journey*, in the questing, in the search for a "better dawn"? What if at times that which can appear as "desolation" is really the *hidden grace of holy Presence*? "The thoughtful nearness to that which seems distant [and often is obfuscated by declarations of certitude] is what our language calls yearning."[6] Holy longing is grace, but it can be excruciating, and because of that, the idols of the past can in our time quite readily take on different power patterns once again. Thus, they can once more endanger our religious quest and hinder us from truly embracing the freedom needed for what elsewhere I have identified as the contemporary movement from "Religion back to Faith"

One goal, then, of my "winter musings," is to reflect on concerns such as these; to do so daringly, and to engage as creatively as possible the very pressing issue of naming and confronting the idols threatening us today—idols that continue to misdirect and obfuscate our search for, and approach to, the Sacred. My hope is that by naming and facing these idols we can reappropriate our freedom as children of God and open ourselves up, once again, to an authentic experience and celebration of Holy Mystery.

THE PSEUDO HOLY

Idols, I believe, present us with the *pseudo holy*—with that which is not authentic but *appears* to be of value, *appears* worthy to be sought after and at times appears even sacred—that which *deceives*. It seems to me that in our time, though we may have done away with golden calves as such, we actually still have a good number of idols. There are, of course, secular ones—related, for the most part, to power, dominance, pleasure, and money. But there are also idols in religion; yes, I believe, even in the Christian/Catholic religion. My concern here is with the Catholic religion.

In one of his best books, in my estimation—*The Fire and the Rose Are One*—Sebastian Moore made an observation that has haunted me to this day. It summarizes the present concerns perfectly: When reflecting on original sin and its debilitating effect on all of us, Moore suggests that it is, in fact, nothing less than *"the unreality of God"*—an unholy, deceitful approach to the Holy. Idols are the signposts of original sin understood in this way. They insist on being taken seriously. They want to be worshipped, and they demand that their worshipers persecute those who ignore them. In our time they are particularly devious since, instead of being seen as opposing the Christian tradition and setting themselves up as counterforces, they actually proclaim it as their base, as their foundation. I believe that this foundation needs to be rattled, as should the idolatrous structure built on it. Four idols seem to me especially relevant for us today:

1. the idol of language, an obsession with correct God-talk, and a naming, particularly, of the Holy One, to serve one's own interests;

2. the idol of gender, which utilizes, in many respects, the idolizing of names to help promote itself;

3. the idol of finality and, with that, permanence, as the hallmark of the sacred;

4. and lastly, the idol of inerrancy.[7]

My choice of these specific idols (for there certainly are others) is because I find them particularly depressing and debilitating for the faith I love. My hope in this reflection is to go to their altars —not for worship, of course, but to rattle them a bit in the hope of opening space, once again, for authentic reverence and awe.

IDOL ONE: LANGUAGE

An obsession with correct God-talk and a naming, specifically, of the Holy Mystery, to serve one's own interests.

I rather doubt that many need clarification here. Language, as we all know, is not irrelevant and arbitrary. "Language," said the philosopher Martin Heidegger, is in fact "the house of Being." By that he wished to indicate that language *speaks* our reality. It provides the home for the articulation of *our* reality and what life means to us. It identifies and names what *is* for us. Heidegger felt that language in Western culture has been so corrupted by rationalism and dualism—(theologically) separating God from God's world—that it has, as he put it, forced the "gods to flee," that is, forced authentic Holiness to *absent* itself. Indeed, Heidegger saw our times as *indigent*—deprived of the most basic necessities for authenticity and the depth desire for the Holy. He speaks of "the *no-more* of the gods that have fled and the *not-yet* of the god to come."[8]

I am reminded here once again of a story I reflected on a number of times, but which bears repeating here. It was told by the Persian mystic Rumi, who writes of Moses overhearing a shepherd at prayer:

> "O God, where are you?" cried the shepherd. "I want to help you, to fix your shoes and comb your hair. I want to wash your clothes and pick the lice off. I want to bring you milk and kiss your little hands and feet when it's time for you to go to bed. I want to sweep your room and keep it neat. God, my sheep and goats are yours. All I can say, remembering you, is Ah!"

Moses couldn't stand it any longer. "Who are you talking to? The one who made us and made the earth and made the sky? Don't talk about shoes and socks with God! And what's this with *your little hands and feet?* Such blasphemous familiarity sounds like you're chatting with your uncles. Only something that grows needs milk. Only someone with feet needs shoes. Not God! . . . This tone [is] foolish and irreverent. . . . Body and birth language are right for us on this side of the river, but not for addressing the origin, not for Allah."

The shepherd repented and tore his clothes, sighed and wandered into the desert.

A sudden revelation came to Moses. God's voice: "you have separated me from one of my own. Did you come as a prophet to unite or to sever? I have given each being a separate and unique way of seeing and knowing and saying that knowledge [i.e., identifying his or her reality].

"What seems wrong to you is right for him. What is poison to one is honey to someone else. Purity and impurity, sloth and diligence in worship, these mean nothing to me. I am apart from all that.

"Ways of worshiping are not to be ranked as better or worse than one another. Hindus do Hindu things. The Dravidian Muslims in India do what they do. It's all praise, and it's all right.

"It's not me that's glorified in acts of worship. It's the worshipers! I don't hear the words they say. I look inside at the humility. That broken-open lowliness is the reality, not the language. Forget phraseology. I want burning, *burning*. Be friends with your burning. Burn up your thinking and your forms of expression! Moses, those who pay attention to ways of behaving and speaking are one sort. Lovers who burn are another."

Rumi tells us that Moses ran after the shepherd and told him that he, Moses, was wrong. "Say whatever or however your loving tells you to. Your sweet blasphemy is the truest devotion. Through you the whole world is freed." The shepherd already was in the depth of mystical union when Moses reached him—united to the Holy One in deepest love.

Rumi ends the story with this admonition: "Whenever you speak praise or thanksgiving to God, [let it always be] like this dear shepherd's simplicity. When you eventually see through the veils to how things really are, you will keep saying over and over again, 'This is certainly not how we thought it was.'"[9]

Reflection

There are a number of ways to reflect on this story. I merely wish to point to the two that I find most pressing:

1. We know today, or at least should know, that all God language is contextual, that it changes with the times, with the culture, even with the individual and his or her limitations of consciousness and situation in the world. We accept that it should be allowed to do this, so that God imagery can be as relevant as possible to the person using it—to his or her gender, race, age, culture, and environment, where alone God can be encountered and where therefore it is possible for revelation to take place. Perhaps no one has expressed this fact more bluntly, but to the point, than the Episcopal bishop John Shelby Spong, who in his book *Why Christianity Must Change or Die* reminds us of the ancient folk wisdom that claims that "if horses had gods they would look like horses." This would, of course, imply that horses had minds that could self-reflect and conceptualize. What Spong wants to point out is that no being can go beyond the limits of its own experience, its own way of being in the world:

> A horse cannot think or imagine beyond the experience of a horse. Despite our human pretensions, that is also true of human beings. If human beings have gods, they will look and act remarkably like human beings. None of us can ever get beyond that. If we are going to speak of God at all, we must begin by acknowledging that limitation. Even if we admit revelation as a source of knowledge, that revelation will be

received and understood within the limits of human experience.[10]

Although this kind of observation has its own shock value and can initially appear disrespectful, might I suggest that those who cannot get beyond the shock and find the comparison offensive, blasphemous perhaps, may not only have shaped God in their own image and likeness but *may want to keep God there for themselves, as well as for everyone else.* Doing that, however, precisely is idol worship and arrogance—as hard as this may be to accept. All God language is metaphor and cannot be otherwise. As such it stands in the tension of "knowing" and "unknowing," of what *is* and what *is not* concerning God. God, as we know, is the absolute Other, absolute Mystery, and anything we say about God is ultimately for our needs, not for God's, and always tentative at best.[11] To absolutize a metaphor is to destroy it's natural tension, insisting on our finite *is*, ignoring the *is not*, and leaving us with idols. Most importantly, it deprives others of *their* symbols by forcing our way of speaking and symbolizing on them and anathematizing anything else.

2. The second lesson we can draw from Rumi's story deals with the *essence* of our God relation and also readies us for considerations concerning idol two: "All I want is burning," God tells Moses. Worship and ritual that fail to lead to this are of no value to God, no matter how aesthetic and majestic or "Latinized" they may be. Pedantic concern about formulations and ritualistic obsessions is

laughable in the face of absolute Mystery, where silent love may be the best form of worship. "I don't *hear the words they say.* I look inside at the humility. That broken-open lowliness is the reality, not the language. Forget phraseology. *I want burning, burning.* Be friends with your burning. Burn up your thinking and your forms of expression! Moses, those who pay attention to ways of behaving and speaking are one sort. Lovers who burn are another." One gets the impression here that Rumi's God finds much of the pedantry (that so often parades as necessary reverence before the Holy One) to be silly at best, but also a waste of time and energy. We need to ask ourselves, therefore, whether it indeed leads us to God or alienates us instead.

IDOL TWO: GENDER

All of us living in these times of awakening conscious-ness regarding the equality and dignity of women will readily see that idol two feeds on idol one. The idol of gender is begotten of an absolutized male image of God and the language that promotes it. On its altar lie the lives and talents, the visions and hopes of women throughout Christendom—all sacrificed (for the sake of power and control) to a patriarchal church and a patriarchal Father,

- who, it is claimed, created the world primarily male and for men,

- whose "misbegotten" creation is woman. Her "unique genius," according to one pope, is either bearing children into the world (preferably male children, I suppose—*in Persona Christi*) or embracing virginity. She is symbolically not fit for ordination, so the gender idolatry will have it, since a woman cannot properly represent Christ (the Bridegroom) to his Bride (the Church).

That the symbology here has been invented, manipulated, and then sanctified by male clerics to their advantage is an example of idol one—shrouded in denial and "sacred" verbiage to which many of us even to this day pay homage, though there really is nothing authentically Christian about this.

"If the symbol oppresses," I suspect Jesus would have said, "get rid of the symbol." Tear it out, like your eye, if it gives scandal. But idols are not that easily done away with, especially if they advantage those in power. And so the sacrificing continues—with excommunications, anathemas, and interdicts even to this day—all, I suppose, to safeguard the Bridegroom and his Bride, Holy Mother Church.

IDOL THREE: PERMANENCE

Idol three: finality, and with that permanence as the hallmark of the sacred, is deeply entrenched in the Catholic psyche. We have:

+ indelible marks,

+ perpetual vows,

- a priesthood forever (ontologically changing a man— whatever that really means beyond the ancient metaphysical category),

- unchanging declarations of dogmatic certitudes,

- and the indissoluble bonds of marriage.

If it is of God—truly holy and good—so the teaching has it, it lasts forever. If it does not, something *has* to have been wrong from the start. The fact that in God's creation the only permanence *is* change has escaped us until now, when the discoveries of science finally invite all of humanity to move beyond Greek metaphysics and the dualistic worldview it master-minded, and to come to grips with transience if we are to face reality *realistically.* In our religious tradition this "coming to grips," however, does not as yet seem to have taken hold:

1. Catholic annulments of marriage still argue that *what was,* really *did not exist,* and so *cannot be binding forever* as *it would if it had actually happened.* One pays good money in honor of idol three and takes it very seriously. Every diocese has its marriage tribunal, frequently administered by clerics serious about the business of deciding the state of conjugal reality.

2. Truth also has frequently been sacrificed at the altar of this idol. *If something is really true, it is so forever,* so the belief has it. And we declare dogmas and doctrines to solidify our explanations of the Christian mysteries for all times, forbidding any questions or reinterpretations

in their regard. How Jesus is God is one example, cast forever in the straightjacket of Hellenic thought. How God is triune, is another. We talk of nature and person: two in one for Jesus, and three in one in reverse for the Trinity. But who today can honestly understand this, find it relevant, and think that it really matters? The idol has obscured the Mystery of love that Trinity reveals to us in God's triple unfolding as creator and loving parent, as redeemer modeling for us the fullness of humanity, and as sanctifier empowering us through the ages. It seems to me that the only ones still talking about all of this are the theologians who get silenced whenever they try too hard to become relevant once again.

At some point in the development of Western thought "truth" became an *object* of knowledge, when *how we know* (epistemology) became equated with *what is as such* (ontology). The objectification of our relationship with and our experience of the world—both in the concrete and in the spiritual sense—turned truth into something final, something over against us, measurable, definable by us, and therefore subject to control. Once we were able to define something we were able to limit it, circumscribe it, and "hold" it in our knowledge. We could control it, and, along with the dictates of idol three, we could ascertain its perpetual validity.

The fact that the worldview that has emerged in the twentieth century (due to the discoveries of science and ongoing quantum research) assures us that there is nothing permanent except change seems to have escaped those in the throes of idol three. Today we know that the reality we encounter *gives itself to us,* largely according to our expectations, in more of an "organic" encounter than a "mechanistic" process, and that it can, therefore, not be seen as permanently definable and objectifyable, but as "relational" instead—an event of self-disclosure, of emergence, of revelation—where the knower and the known are intertwined, as it were, in a dance of ever greater and deeper "presencing."

The effects that these twentieth-century insights have had on the scientific community have been cataclysmic, to say the least, and the upheaval in our scientific approach to the world of reality is still being dealt with. Religion in many respects, however, seems to have chosen the "ostrich approach" and, with numerous evasions of the issue, is holding on in perpetuity regardless of the growing irrelevance of some of its declarations, which have become at best confusing and at worst incomprehensible to the community of believers. Here idol three is aided, conveniently, by idol four.

IDOL FOUR: INERRANCY

Since idol four guarantees inerrancy, those who adhere to it need not worry about contextualizing, that is, making the "truths" of our tradition intelligible and culturally as well as linguistically meaningful to the twentieth-century believer. The doctrines and dogmas declared through the ages (as well as some longstanding beliefs of the Christian community considered part of sacred tradition) hold us bound, whether we understand them or not. Regardless of the motivation or the historical context out of which any of these arose, they impose themselves on us simply by virtue of their declared holiness, which, with the help of idol three, guarantees them in perpetuity, no matter what alternate discoveries and insights have arisen since their declaration. We blithely fit the corpse to the coffin, so to speak, even if we have to cut off its head. *The symbolism here may be more apropos than intended.*

Perhaps some examples will clarify our dilemma, even if they make us uncomfortable:

The Dogma of the Immaculate Conception: It was declared in 1854 by Pope Pius IX—just about all by himself, as some scholars maintain. He seems to have ignored the views of eminent Christian theologians present and past, notably Thomas Aquinas, Bonaventure, and his predecessor, Pope Gregory XVI, and declared the dogma without any meaningful discussion with the church's body of bishops. He required them, instead, and all the faithful with them, to accept this dogma simply because the pontiff had so declared it.[12]

Through his purportedly single-handed declaration of the Immaculate Conception, Pope Pius IX (perhaps unintentionally or without forethought) changed an almost two-thousand-year-old belief that human life begins at "ensoulment"—some forty to eighty days after conception. By positing this dogma, the pope unilaterally declared that the beginning of Mary's life, her "ensoulment" as human, occurred at her conception. Thus, without any meaningful consultation, he altered "in perpetuity" the Catholic position on abortion, which then had to adapt, regardless of previous Christian beliefs, or for that matter, scientific opinions that differ to this day: "In the 1869 constitution *Apostolicae sedis,* Pius IX simply revised the existing penalty for abortion (excommunication) by omitting the reference to the 'ensouled fetus.' He considered abortions the same at any stage of pregnancy, implying immediate ensoulment,"[13] and opening moral arguments regarding abortion as well as contraception to this day. (My example of the church's changing and often unilateral and doctrinaire positions, in this case on early abortion, needs to be taken as related to the matter under discussion, not as an endorsement of abortion as such.) Perhaps the most disturbing aspect of this example, and my primary reason for presenting it, is the lack of consultation on the part of pontifical leadership with the bishops of the time, with medical research, or simply with the tradition as such. *That* might, at least, have elicited some hesitation about making pronouncements unilaterally and in the pope's view "infallibly."

Consultation and serious dialogue with those who have alternative or simply new views seem to be a major deficiency in the Catholic Church. Even Pope Paul VI's attempt to revisit the issue of contraception (affirming Pope John XXIII's calling together a commission of experts on this subject, including some married people) was short-circuited by a small minority of the commission who pointed out to the pontiff that the ordinary Magisterium of the church had upheld the belief that contraception must be avoided and was a serious sin and that, therefore, the matter should be beyond further discussion. Paul VI accepted this view, disregarding his commission's majority report, and came out with the encyclical *Humane Vitae,* which caused an immediate and unprecedented negative reaction among Catholics. As Hans Küng observes in his short historical study *The Catholic Church*: "*Humane Vitae* was the first instance in the church history of the twentieth century when the vast majority of people and clergy refused obedience to the pope in an important matter, though in the papal view this was in fact an infallible teaching."[14] Many Catholics today simply ignore it, rejecting, in this regard, ecclesial leadership as unmindful of their reality and as claiming even greater certainty than science does about a biological question.

I return now to the dogma of the Immaculate Conception of Mary to identify yet another example of idols three and four: claiming that Mary from the moment of her conception was free from original sin which, as the teaching has it and this dogma affirms, is inherited by

all other humans through the sexual pleasure (concupis-
cence) of our parents during intercourse.[15] The fact that
inheriting original sin through the sexual pleasure experienced in the conjugal act does not speak meaningfully
to Catholics of today leaves us in the *truth* quandary I
mentioned earlier (idol three: If something is really true,
it must be permanently so). We are told that a dogma of
the church is truth, and as such it should be held by all
the forever (idol four). Reformulating, let alone reversing
it, should therefore be out of the question, since infallibility guarantees it in perpetuity. In the case of original
sin, theologians in modern times certainly have struggled with its meaning, and done so perhaps with greater
freedom than more recent statements claiming infallibility regarding other issues have allowed. Nevertheless, ordinary Catholic couples even today, faced with
an "under-explained" theology of baptism, still worry
mightily and feel pressed to have their child baptized,
especially in the case of illness.

Limbo (which by two previous councils had even
been replaced with a milder form of hell)[16] has, thank
God, been officially done away with twice now in the
last fifty years. It was dismissed first, by implication, in
the theology of Vatican II,[17] and second, by Pope Bene-
dict XVI in 2007. Nevertheless, the notion of "inheriting"
original sin seems to survive due to the lack of an equally
extensive and official "cleansing" of this notion for ordinary Catholics in general—a proof that idols three and
four still linger on.

HISTORICAL CONUNDRUM

The struggle with infallibility and the permanence it imposes on subsequent generations has been painful ever since its inception. History, however, seems to belie the reality of permanence, inerrancy, and doctrinal purity. Councils of the past have been known to condemn popes for heresies,[18] and popes have even excommunicated each other.[19] Perhaps most interesting for our reflection is the fact that some five hundred years before infallibility was formally pronounced a dogma, it was declared a heresy.

Papal infallibility was Pius IX's primary reason for calling Vatican Council I. Historians tell us that he would not and could not accept disagreement on this matter. He pushed so hard for his perspective that at the end about a third of the bishops attending the council actually went home in protest and did not come back for the final vote.[20] Pope John XXII, on the other hand, in the bull *Quia Quorundam* in 1324 declared infallibility a "pestiferous doctrine . . . pernicious audacity." He saw it as "a limitation of his rights as a sovereign" and condemned it "as the work of the devil."[21]

Given these inconsistencies and clear disagreements between pontiffs and the doubt they place on the perpetuity of truth as well as on the infallibility of pontifical statements, one could certainly wonder who should have acquiesced to whom in dealing with this particular topic. If the formal pronouncements of popes are infallible how does one deal with contradictory pronouncements? The fact that only intense research allows one to discover the historical confusion related to permanence and infallibility in the church does make me wonder whether these dogmas are at times being used merely for ecclesial convenience. Why, for example, would John XXII's declaration or the interdicts against the teachings of popes by councils not have been identified as potential historical stumbling blocks to the dogma of infallibility? And why is all of this buried in historical texts rarely read by the laity who, nevertheless, are bound by papal pronouncements under pain of sin? Was there, perhaps, the feeling that few would notice historical contradictions?

The argument can of course be made, and has in fact been made, that infallibility applies only to ex cathedra statements and that this concept did not exist until the sixteenth century. From this position, then, the popes before that time never spoke infallibly. It is difficult, therefore, to bind infallibility to history, but it is also convenient, since it seemingly sweeps away the need to explain the condemnation for heresy of Pope Honorarius I (610–38) by three ecumenical councils.[22] The ex cathedra requisite can also conveniently help the proponents of papal infallibility to ignore the papal bull of John XXII in 1324 against it. The problem is therefore solved by denying retroactivity. But are we not courting the absurd to claim by our "ex cathedra restrictions" that infallibility was necessary only after the mid eighteen hundreds and that the guidance of the church was not a serious matter before then? For educated Catholics what is really very sad can become almost laughable. But the relevance of our tradition is really not a laughing matter. The credibility of the church's leadership is at stake, and the seeming disregard for truly holy wisdom seems scandalous. The examples mentioned so far have led to ruined marriages and families, kept women "in their place," and destroyed their health and well-being in numerous ways, particularly through endless childbearing. They have instilled fear and stifled debate, research, and Catholic scholarship for centuries.

4

BECAUSE WE HAVE NEVER DONE IT

The soul does not have illumination, except when considering the church in relation to the times.

—Saint Bonaventure

A primary example of the pain and confusion experienced by Catholics today due to the idols we are rattling here is the diminishment in their access to the sacraments, especially the Eucharist, the closing of their parish churches, and the dispersion of their communities due to a shortage of priests. Ancient regulations are infallibly upheld (ex cathedra or not) without viable explanations. As statistics seem to indicate, the majority of Catholics today see these as irrelevant and meaningless but seem angry and helpless to change anything.

Perhaps no story addressing this dilemma is more to the point than the one found in John Allen's, blog for the *National Catholic Reporter* (June 27, 2011). Here the revered Cardinal José da Cruz Policarpo, patriarch of Lisbon, Portugal, is reported to have declared in an interview with a legal publication in Portugal called *Oa* that there exists "no fundamental theological obstacle to the ordination of women as priests in the Catholic Church," and that the reticence to do so was more a question of "tradition" since it had "never been done." He suggested that the tradition came "from Jesus and from the fact that the churches of the Reformation conceded the priesthood to women." The cardinal claimed that in the Catholic Church it would happen "only when God wants it," but that that time had not yet come, "because of 'the series of reactions' it would generate." He also suggested that the "young women" in his acquaintance who argue for the ordination of women are generally not interested in becoming priests themselves. The argument, he claimed, is therefore a "false problem."

A number of questions come to my mind in the light of the NCR report: I must admit that I found it astounding that, given the "official" Catholic climate of today, a cardinal would actually make remarks such as these, especially in the immediate aftermath of the punitive action taken by the administration in Rome against the Australian bishop William Morris of Toowoomba, who suggested that dialogue concerning the ordination of women might be helpful. There also have been punitive actions, excommunications, and interdicts imposed on others who have publicly supported this position. I certainly admire the cardinal's courage in saying what he did but sense that his observations as a whole invite further reflection and that the issue of excluding women from ordination needs to be viewed in a wider perspective than the one offered by him.

To begin with, I must admit that I am baffled at how anyone, including a cardinal or even a pope, can unabashedly make declarative statements about what "God wants." I cannot help thinking of the "God and Job exchange" in the Hebrew scriptures, and God's challenge to Job, who seemed to claim an understanding of God's ways: "Where were you," God asks Job (*Where were any of us?*), "when I laid the foundations of the earth?. . . Tell me if you have *understanding. . . .* Have you *comprehended* the expanse of the earth? . . . Declare *if you know all this*" (Job 38:4–18). Does Job have even the slightest capacity to *know* the "*why*" of God's actions? Who, in other words, can *truly know the mind of God*?

To quote directly as NCR reports it: The cardinal suggests that the ordination of women will happen "'when God wants it,' although not in our lifetime, and that now is not the time to raise the question." How, I wonder, has God communicated this to him? Is there possibly an assumption that the discernment of a cardinal carries more weight with God than that of a growing number of the laity—the *sensus fidelium*? If so, where or how can such a conviction be defended theologically with any credibility? Declarations, even those made by persons of great importance, need to be substantiated for credibility. Simply saying something, no matter how often or how loudly, does not make a statement true. Even the dogma of papal infallibility has criteria attached to it, though they may not always be observed. How, then, can any *human* being pronounce himself or herself with certainty concerning the "will of God"? From what source does the cardinal get this insight? Is there really anything other than the reason that "we have never done it" that he is relying on?

It seems difficult to fathom that a man of the cardinal's stature and theological background is not aware of the reasons why this was never done. Does he not recognize the cultural misogyny that has prevailed during and after the life of Jesus? Has he not read any of the numerous scholarly exegeses that show how, in fact, Jesus (most assuredly the one by whose example we should all live) resisted such antagonism in his own day and modeled a gender inclusive manner of relating? If Jesus is the church's model of how we are to relate to the Divine and how the Divine relates to us, how can anyone, let alone a respected cardinal, claim the "will of God" for the church's intransigence regarding the ordination of women?

I find it interesting that when one studies the life of Jesus, one finds that exclusion of any kind was clearly a behavior eschewed by him. His all-inclusive table fellowship is hailed consistently by scripture scholars, who generally see it as, indeed, a major reason for the strong antagonism toward him among the Jewish priests of his day. He kept company with gentiles and with "Jews who acted like gentiles." He ate with sinners and outcasts, with rich and poor, clean and unclean, women and men. As John Dominic Crossan observes so well: where Jesus ate, anyone could be observed reclining at table next to anyone else—a mode of behavior that caused major social scandal and disdain in his day.[23] Jesus, we are told, did not explicitly pronounce himself *against* the social rules of exclusion; he simply *ignored* them. He was persecuted for his behavior, of course, and so are those who ignore the rules of exclusion prevalent in the Catholic Church today. The women who have ignored them and have allowed themselves to be validly (even if not licitly) ordained as Catholic priests have been excommunicated and maligned. Those who support them are forced to resign from their official church ministries if they do not submit and publicly lie about their convictions.

What does the statement that "now is not the time" mean then? Is it impractical? Would too many persons be upset by it? Would the present magisterial church be uncomfortable with it or inconvenienced into explaining its rational and the plethora of historical data concerning the exclusion of women and their persecution throughout its reign? How would Jesus who, as the Story is interpreted, missioned a woman to be the "apostle to the apostles," have dealt with the issue of church closings and sacramental deprivation due to the decline in the clerical caste? What would he say about the denial of call? Why should anyone be deprived of table fellowship, of the sacred meal, and the experience of the Body of Christ and how can that possibly be excused by claiming that "now is not the time"? If not now, then when?

The second issue that comes to mind as I ponder the cardinal's statement goes even deeper and touches the official claims made and interpretations given concerning the sacrament of holy orders. I find myself wondering whether the cardinal's rejection of any valid theological argument against women's ordination might not also open up the question into the historical and theologically convenient claim about the validity of men's ordination, especially if one takes as one's starting point and rationale the activity of Jesus. As disturbing as this might be, does not the evidence of biblical scholarship clearly cast doubt on the claim that, *anyone* was "ordained" by Jesus at the Last Supper? It seems to me and, I suspect, to many who thoughtfully consider this topic both exegetically and historically, that "the sacrament of ordination," at least *as we understand it today,* never happened at *any time* during the life of Jesus. Priesthood was really not on his "agenda," nor does there seem to be any evidence that it was addressed in the early years of the "Jewish-Christian movement" after his death and resurrection. Jesus, it is well known, was a faithful Jew who had major issues with the priestly caste of his religion. They, after all, were ultimately responsible for handing him over to his Roman executioners. Jesus was a faithful Jew and a "lay" person, to use today's language; so were all of his disciples, as well as the apostle Paul.

According to the sacramental theologian Kenan Osborne, as well as Professor Herbert Haag (Lucerne and Tübingen), to mention just two experts on this issue, the earliest references to the ordination of priests in the Christian tradition occurred somewhere around the beginning of the third century.[24] The breaking of the bread and sharing of table fellowship in memory of Jesus was, of course, an established Christian practice that started shortly after Jesus' earthly life and, therefore, existed well before the official ordination of priests took place. The Jewish followers of Jesus were known for commensality and free healing, but the official establishment of a "religion" separate from Judaism really did not happen until sometime after the Jewish revolt against Rome and the destruction of the Temple in Jerusalem at the end of the first century.

I find the cardinal's remarks about the "tradition" dating back to the time of Jesus, therefore, puzzling at best. Jesus, I cannot stress enough, was a Jew, and if the Last Supper was, in fact, the Passover celebration (as it is depicted in the Synoptic Gospels though not clearly in John), it has to be understood as such. It was a covenant meal celebrated by Jesus and his followers in the Jewish tradition. It included taking, blessing, breaking, and sharing bread and, at the end of the meal, blessing and sharing a cup of wine in memory of their covenant with God, who liberated the Jewish people out of Egypt and with whom (through this communal act of sharing) they understood themselves as one in thanksgiving and in commitment to God's law.

We believe that Jesus broadened that covenant with new insights as to who this God is for us, and what God asks of us. We believe that the disciples understood his message. They had, after all, lived it with him throughout his public ministry, and so, when they gathered after the resurrection experience, they celebrated this new covenant for which their leader had died, and for which many of them, and many after them, would live and eventually die as well.

There is still a third question that arises for me as I reflect on the cardinal's opinion that the time for women's ordination is not now, though *theologically* there is really no reason against it. I wonder whether his statement could not also call into question (intentionally or not) the claim to infallibility in this regard purportedly made by Pope John Paul II and reemphasized by the present pontiff? If the cardinal is correct in saying that there are no *theological* reasons against the ordination of women, then where does the infallibility regarding the papal ban on it (as well as the ban on discussing this issue) find its justification? It seems to me improbable that any pontiff would claim infallibility for any declaration outside the theological realm, since that would at best be reaching into the absurd.

If my recollection serves me right, the matter of infallibility regarding the ban on women's ordination arose after 1994 and the publication of Pope John Paul's apostolic letter *Ordinatio Sacerdotalis* ("On Reserving

Priestly Ordination to Men Alone"). It would appear that some commentators wanted to know whether the claim that the church did not have power to ordain women and that the matter should now be closed to discussion was an infallible statement. The Congregation for the Doctrine of the Faith replied for the pontiff in the affirmative. Up to the present time, however, it seems that the Magisterium has stopped short of claiming "divine revelation" as its justification, though the cardinal's statement that women's ordination is not *God's will at this time* does court this kind of overreaching.

It certainly is interesting that, in spite of the papal declaration, discussion around this topic continues unabated among Catholic scholars and among an ever increasing number of the Catholic laity (who are seriously disadvantaged by this ruling in many respects), rendering the "infallibility" issue in this regard (and, by extension, in general) progressively irrelevant. (The same disregard, as I mentioned earlier, is shown today, as statistics indicate, by numerous Catholics throughout the world with respect to Pope Paul VI's Encyclical: *Humanae Vitae* and its prohibition on contraception.) In the nineteenth century, Lord Acton (a leading Catholic and a British historian, who succeeded Cardinal Newman as the editor of the Catholic periodical *The Rambler* and was known for his opposition to the theory of papal infallibility) is purported to have made the statement that "there is no worse heresy than the fact that the office sanctifies the holder of it." For that very reason, any church doctrine or discipline—no matter how sacred it is claimed to be magisterially—if it advantages the ruling "cast" at the expense of the entire people of God and claims infallibility or even the Divine will itself as its defense, should undergo serious scrutiny and criticism. And this, I suggest, should be executed by a body larger than and independent of the internal forum.

INTERLUDE: ENCOUNTERING ONE'S OWN REALITY

While I was struggling with these thoughts, finding them puzzling and upsetting on many levels, I had a dream. It came quite unexpectedly, as dreams quite naturally do, and was exceedingly painful:

I found myself with my two sisters and my mother in a hotel somewhere in a large city. It was Sunday, but none of my family seemed interested in going to church. The atmosphere between us (quite uncharacteristically) was indifferent—perhaps even somewhat hostile. I decided to go to Mass by myself and headed to the cathedral nearby. Instead of finding the usual worship space, however, I found what looked more like a dining room. Tables were arranged in a large square and mostly elderly women religious (some in habit) were sitting there eating but also waiting for the priest (to preside). Chairs that were not occupied were nevertheless reserved for others, and I found it difficult to find a place. I finally left, feeling like an unwelcome intruder.

Outside it had started to rain heavily and was pitch dark, making it impossible to see anything. I knew that there was traffic, and I feared getting hit by the cars, which I heard but could not see. Something inside me reassured me that I would not be hurt, as I had yet "much more work to do." When the weather cleared, I was totally lost and seemed to have some odd kind of amnesia concerning my surroundings. I was in a place with numerous churches but could find neither the hotel nor the cathedral. There were some friendly strangers (women) who tried to help me find the cathedral. We looked into one church where there were a number of priests standing around the altar and wearing tiaras. I observed unkindly that they all wanted to be kings. The women laughed.

Nothing was familiar, and I was thoroughly confused. I had nothing but my cell phone with me and tried to call a friend in my hometown to help me get my family's phone numbers, but I found myself incapable of dialing the number. The feeling of total lost-ness and alienation was overwhelming and I woke up with a sick feeling in my heart—exhausted.

MUSINGS

When cultures are in turmoil and a major shift in consciousness is taking place, the feeling of alienation and lost-ness is often inevitable. This is exacerbated among the members of the community when fear hinders those in leadership positions from listening to creative and unexpected voices, in other words, from engaging in dialogue and embracing change. They cling instead to the familiar, the tried and true of former times, declaring it holy and sacrosanct and denouncing everything that might disturb the secure and cherished status quo.

My dream, I believe, was so disturbing to me because the normal symbols of security and support—family, religious congregation, church—presented themselves as alien or foreclosed to me, and any contact with them was made impossible. What felt like a suffocating form of amnesia left me fearing total annihilation. I sensed that I no longer belonged, that my place in this world was gone. Clearly, the "old" (tiaras and clerical kingship) felt alienating, even laughable, and totally out of step— a caricature of the *Persona Christi* who emerges from our Gospel stories. My sense of what ought to replace it, however (namely, an all inclusive Eucharistic meal), also was out of sync. It seemed exclusive in its self-centeredness (all the chairs were occupied or reserved) and was therefore denied to me. In both cases I walked away and left them behind.

Yet the dream's message in the face of imminent danger (darkness, rain, and the sound of traffic coming toward me) was that "I had work to do" and that no fatal harm would come to me even from unseen sources. The apparent collapse of everything around me and my inability to connect with everything that had seemed important to me, was not only confusing, but also thoroughly terrifying.

It occurred to me, as I pondered the dream, especially its timing—happening, as it did, shortly after I had written the above reflection—that the hesitation and the stress I had felt while writing it, though I would not allow these to deter me from expressing my concerns, nevertheless had entered into my "dream world." They were reminding me of the hurt that a structure, such as the Magisterium of my church, can inflict on those whose love for the mission of Jesus compels them to question what appear to be unfounded and often oppressive policies and dicta. Our sacred Story has it that Jesus warned that those who would put family first—father, mother, brothers, and sisters—could not be his disciples. His was a demand, I believe, to establish priorities rather than to reject those we love. Following the vision of Jesus demands total and uncompromised commitment to the Quest, no matter how culturally or ecclesially unpopular and personally inconvenient and painful this may be.

The dilemma of today, then, is grave: We either agree to return to the "pastor and flock" mentality of pre-Vatican II, and Pius X's observation that: "the only duty of the multitude is to allow themselves to be led, and, like a docile flock, to follow the pastors" (*Vehementer Nos*), or we must accept that, in our age, speaking one's views and voicing one's questions are clearly the marks of loyal faithfulness rather than betrayal. As Donald Cozzens observes:

> Catholics today are among the best-educated and theologically astute sociological groups in the world. They bristle when it is suggested that they should allow themselves to be led like a docile flock of sheep by their pastors.[25]

Cozzens entitled the book from which this citation is derived: *Faith That Dares to Speak.* For today's Catholic, the love of Christ impels each and all of us to do just that.

"LORD, WHERE SHALL WE GO?"

Our reflections so far have no doubt been uncomfortable and even painful. I have come to believe that this is so because idols have a tendency to threaten authenticity and depth. They are self-serving, impose punishments on those who question or ignore them, and deny the Mystery. What then can be done to reverence that Mystery once again and to come home to our deepest longing? Let me, in conclusion, offer just a few suggestions.

Idol One: Language
Idol Two: Gender

Language used idolatrously destroys the sacred and negates an authentic connection to the Mystery. That this has happened and is happening in our church is beyond question. Historically, the dualistic language of our Church and the worship style entrenched in it has offered us ever more limited access to the Divine. This limitation has been felt ever more acutely in proportion to our gaining a sense of our own identity through theological education and reflection, and I am talking here especially of women and the laity as a whole, whom hierarchism and gynophobia have oppressed for centuries.

The retrieval of authentic God talk is essential in our time. This cannot be reactionary, however, but rather must flow from the burning that Rumi taught us about in his shepherd story. It is my belief that for this to happen, a gentle retrieval of the *apophatic* (silence and awe in our worship) may be very helpful. Taizé seems to have the right recipe here. And I am amazed at how the Taizé approach attracts young people from all over the world. Music and sharing of the word interspersed with long periods of silent listening to the inner voice of Love would do much to have us reconnect to the Sacred.

This, of course, will require some getting used to. The rites of the church today seem to me centered much too much on proper ritual and correct language—on words, words, and more words. And so I suggest that the antidote to the idolatry of language could be simple and reverent silence. In our tradition this is called the *apophatic* approach, which emphasizes the lack of adequate language for the Divine. It must be stressed, of course, that the *apophatic* is not simply silence. It is silence, rather, that flows out of speechlessness in the face of ineffable Love. We are overwhelmed by the Mystery, and words fail us. The *apophatic* arises from humility and awe.

This disposition eschews the legislation of divine names—the acceptance of some and rejection of others. There are *no* names that are adequate, and what we say comes straight out of our poverty as well as our human and finite need. When we speak, our words are therefore rooted in silence and return us ultimately to silence. This is the stuff of depth prayer and God-connectedness. Prayer experiences and liturgical rites that reverence stillness and encourage a naming and praising of the Holy One that arise out of that stillness are of tremendous value in this age of transforming consciousness.

Inclusive language at all official prayer experiences should also be common practice. Liturgy is *for the assembly* of women and men. It is the prayer of the Body. For those who *see* with new eyes, inclusive language is not a favor to women dependent on the benevolence of the presider. It is a matter of courtesy and justice.

Idol Three: Permanence
Idol Four: Inerrancy

Idols three, permanence, and four, inerrancy, need special attention, since they are directly related to a major shift in worldviews that is happening upon us. I believe it is the most significant shift in human consciousness perhaps since the agricultural revolution, some ten thousand years ago, perhaps in all time.

Briefly to review what I have touched on already and written about in other books: We know from science today that change is ongoing and is good. Without it there would be no growth, no advancement, no maturation and development either physically or spiritually. Science, in fact, tells us that there is in this universe nothing permanent except change.

But with the disappearance of permanence also goes the demise of static truth and, therefore, of infallibility and once and for all dogmatic certitudes. They were built (and I do not want to belabor this) on the Hellenic worldview of antiquity that later, through enculturation, was adopted by Christianity. It divided the universe into two realities: one of spirit and the other of matter, with the first, stable, reliable, and ultimately of God; the second, fickle and unreliable—the source of suffering and evil, to be avoided as much as possible by all of us aspiring to eternal salvation.

This worldview, the source of idealism and materialism and what is generally referred to as dualism, has been with us in various ways since the agricultural revolution some ten thousand years ago, but got a major boost with Hellenic metaphysics and in later years with the rationalism and empiricism of what is now referred to as the modern era. It collapsed ever so reluctantly and with great scientific trauma at the beginning of the twentieth century (not that any of us were much aware of it, and present religious leadership still does not seem to be). It came to an end with the scientific discoveries of Einstein and then of quantum physics.[26]

The quantum perspective, new insights in astro-physics, in physics, and in biology generally and the influence these should have on spirituality came to the awareness of spiritual writers some time in the latter part of the twentieth century (with the exception of the earlier mystical writings of paleontologist Teilhard de Chardin). Their importance for us lies in the fact that they radically open up and challenge our God perspective, calling not for rejection, but for deeper insight. They invite us today to ponder deeply, to provide for the people of God new pos-sibilities, to take a hold of our maturity, to shed the dia-pers of dependence, to take on personal responsibility in our God quest, and to ask our leadership to do the same.

We are, in our time, gifted with everything it takes to be creative stewards of this evolving world and the wonder it offers us for our celebration, meditation, and reflection. Science, in spite of the fact that organized reli-gion even to this day is still holding it at arms length, is today, in many of its disciplines

1.   beginning to acknowledge mystery,

2.   pointing us to the elegance of creation,

3.   calling us to respect and reverence,

4.   pointing, through its discoveries, unquestionably to our interdependence, and

5.   inviting us to deepen our sense of community.

We are today beginning to experience communion—not just among humans but, as I discussed elsewhere already[27] amazingly, with all of creation. We are
beginning to take seriously that we are cosmically interconnected. The mechanistic, dualistic, and often hierarchical approach to creation is being challenged, and we
are being invited to see the cosmos as a living organism
with mysterious principles of order and mind.

These insights call for a new depth response. What
may appear at first to undermine tradition and creed
needs to be explored as relevant to contemporary religion. Old and unchanging laws need not only to be reap-
praised and rethought, but also to be reformulated and
integrated. All this needs to take place (and this is where
the difficulty comes in, and all of us have to take responsibility) within a faith system that, as I have pointed out,
has preached permanence ever since, as a missionary
movement it accepted the Greek worldview close to two
thousand years ago, a faith system that abhors change as
fickle and unreliable and has created dogmas to assure
solidity and declare infallibility.

Transformation, then, is a mammoth task! And
today it behooves all of us to be on the forefront of this
transformation, to be about it with love and also with
respect for what was. Respect, however, does not mean
acquiescence, nor intransigence. It means gratitude for
the strivings of the past, but also thoughtful and communal questioning into the appropriateness of this past for

today. It means bringing about life-giving change when necessary for the well-being of the community. It means theological reflection that connects with the findings of other disciplines and accepts cultural development as necessary and good. We stand on the shoulders of those who came before us not to rest there, but rather to see and move beyond their vision into an ever greater unfolding of the Mystery.

We live in times of extraordinary change, where knowledge no longer belongs to a chosen few but is available to all of us who are willing; where in a sense truth has become "democratic" and is within the purview of anyone willing to search, study, and explore. As I mentioned already: *the agony as well as the ecstasy is in the journey,* and all of us are on the road with the assurance that the Spirit of God continues to unfold in our midst, that creation and redemption are ongoing, and that the Christ event has resources up to now untapped, and is calling all of us, as Christ's Body, to new ways of understanding hitherto unheard of.

THOUGHTS AND QUESTIONS
FOR MEDITATION

1. What is your reaction to the "what if" questions at the beginning of chapter 3, paragraph three: "But what if the infidel and worshipper of idols is to be found not so much as the one who does not accept, or consider as important, some of the long-held religious truths of any particular faith system *but is, instead, the enforcer of the creed*?" and the rest of the paragraph? Do you agree with the questions' attempt to "turn the tables," so to speak. If so, why?

2. "What if the ecstasy is, in fact, primarily *in the journey*, in the questing, in the search for a 'better dawn'?" "What if at times that which can appear as 'desolation' is really the *hidden grace of holy Presence*?" How do you understand this question?

3. In the section entitled "The Pseudo Holy," I suggest that the idols are the signposts of original sin understood the way Sebastian Moore defines it. What does that mean to you?

4. What has been your experience of the idol of language? How has it been debilitating for your God quest? What is your reaction to the statement that *all*, yes, ALL God language is metaphor and depends on the context of its time?

5. Do you find the reflection on idol two extreme or right on. Why?

6. Why do you think idol three, permanence, has been so important to Christianity. How do you react to the statement that it is in fact an idol?

7. What is your reaction to the observations by Cardinal José da Cruz Policarpo, patriarch of Lisbon, Portugal, reported in the *National Catholic Reporter* (June 27, 2011)? How do you react to the various points raised about the cardinal's position in this chapter? Do any of them strike you as particularly pertinent or surprising?

8. "When cultures are in turmoil and a major shift in consciousness is taking place, the feeling of alienation and lost-ness is often inevitable. This is exacerbated among the members of the community when fear hinders those in leadership positions from listening to creative and unexpected voices, from engaging in dialogue and embracing change. They cling instead to the familiar—the tried and true of former times, declaring it holy and sacrosanct and denouncing everything that might disturb the secure and cherished status quo." Does this statement from the section entitled " Musings" resonate with your experience?

9. What is your reaction to the "dilemma of today" as it is described at the end of chapter 4 in the section entitled "Musings"?

10. Respond to the suggestions offered in response to the four idols discussed in chapters 3 and 4 under the heading, "Lord, Where Shall We Go?" Do you have other suggestions?

Part Three

GOD IN OUR MIDST

Chapter 5
A Dream

Chapter 6
What About Salvation?

Chapter 7
On Being the Body

5

A DREAM

God's voice is the call of transcendence that challenges us to go further, to do more, to try harder, to change our lives, to venture out into new areas and into the unknown. God is out there calling us to move . . . beyond our narrow and limited ideas of what is possible. —Albert Nolan

It was early morning—the day before Christmas Eve. I woke up from a dream and could not go back to sleep: I was in a classroom full of young adults, one of whom had asked me to address directly this question: "Did Jesus come to save us?" I remember sensing urgency in his request that, somehow, would not be satisfied with equivocation or vagueness. The ordinary, or perhaps the "simple" answer to his question is of course: "yes." We profess this "yes" in our creeds and celebrate it in the great feasts of our liturgical year (a major one of which had very likely invited this question into my dream world just now). I knew, however, that this student of mine — a symbol of myself, no doubt—wanted more.

At first I was somewhat taken aback by his question, not because I doubted the place of Jesus as Savior in the

Christian dispensation, but because I felt the question had come from a deeper place in this young man than the simple story of our Christmas parable. I was, however, not quite ready to answer it just yet. After some moments of silence during which years of pondering this topic coursed through my head, I decided first to turn the question over to the class and see what they thought. Mine was not an attempt to escape and surrender this moment to the light banter of a "coffee-*klatsch*" or opinion survey. It came rather, and urgently I might add, out of a hope to discover how far my students had moved in their own reflection on this topic, and how ready they were for a deeper plunge into the wonder of the Christian Mystery. With that question, however, I awoke and the dream, but not its challenge, ended.

MUSINGS

As synchronicity would have it, I had received a gift on the day before the dream "came to me." It was a lovely little book and CD by Mary Lowry, titled *Mary Did You Know*—a meditation on the strength and vision of Mary as she faced the destiny of her Son as Savior. The cover of the book indicated that it had sold 650,000 copies. Very likely the book and CD, and my reaction to them at this time of year, had helped bring about my dream, and so I am sitting here, pondering.

In spite of my alarm at the commercial frenzy into which the pre-Christmas season has degenerated, and my aversion to the "ardent" admonitions from every possible media source that we spend money to help create jobs and save a perilous economy, there is still for me something very tender and heartwarming about how we depict the Story we celebrate on December 25. We long for family and friends during this time and reach out to those who are lonely and deprived of love and of the basic necessities of life. That, in many respects, is for me the beauty of this season. After all, Christmas gifts, whether many of us remember this or not, were initially intended to remind us of *the* gift of God in Christ Jesus; and our generosity toward those in need is the way we give thanks for God's bounty and mercy toward us. The love and care we are invited to show to others during this time, therefore, is meant as a response of gratitude:

> "Whatever you do to the least of my brothers and sisters, you do to me."

We prepare for Christmas during four weeks of waiting, called Advent—a term implying "the coming," not just of the Christ *Child* but, more significantly, of what this Child's birth implies, namely, the coming of Christ *as Savior*. The entire Christian Story (and that, for us, means a story intended for humankind as a whole) is wrapped up, then, in a deep and powerful love manifestation that extends far beyond the actual birth of Jesus.

It has become clear to me over the years and came back to me again while pondering the dream that what we celebrate in Christ's birth is indeed the *core*

of our Christian faith. Is not all of Christianity primarily about God birthing God's self into our very midst?
God's presence in Jesus focuses our faith. It is *the* message, therefore, because without what we have come to
call "incarnation" there really would be no Christianity. And this, if seen in the light of the transformation of
consciousness that the new "universe story" is opening
up for us in our time is not *just* because Jesus was born,
and in him God was manifest and became one with us
in a very special and unique way. It is really because *in*
Jesus of Nazareth, a human being very much like us,
what already was reached a climax. The Jesuit scholar
Roger Haight says it well when he points out that "it is no
less than God with whom we are confronted in Jesus."[28]
Jesus, then, in his humanity, in his presence in history,
in his life lived fully in the service of Love, witnessed to
the fullness of God and made this fullness available to
us who share in this humanity. There is a passion in all
of this: the passion of a God who so loved us as to make
us a conscious part of the extraordinary event of divine
self-presencing in creation, which in Jesus became most
fully manifest.

As we enter into this realization and make it our
own, it is important that our attention be focused on
Jesus as a *human being*, a *creature like us.* This *is*, after all,
what connects him to us and us to him, and what allows
for our eventual and blissful realization that, since our
faith tells us that God, indeed, was fully manifest in the

human Jesus, God can be manifest in us as well. What this means is that we who are human beings can be God-bearers also, and that the purpose of God's self-presencing in Jesus is to reveal to all of humanity that our fulfillment, the actual destiny of humankind and its salvation, *is* divinization. We all believe that God sent God's Son, that the birth of Jesus is what incarnation is all about. What I am proposing here, however, is that incarnation is even bigger than that, that *all of us* are involved in it. We, together with all of creation, are part of it—not merely as beneficiaries and therefore somehow as spectators "outside" of the event as such, but rather as *in* it, as part of it and belonging to it.

WHAT WE WERE TAUGHT

Thoughts such as these can be confusing and even frightening at first. They can certainly move us beyond long-held and traditional strictures and propel us into *wonder.* This can, of course, be disturbing for some (especially for Catholics) because we have been accustomed to think that once dogmas and doctrines have been declared, there is not much room for wondering anymore. Some of the declarations of the past may have sounded strange to us at times, but we did not want to doubt, and for many of us that generally meant that we did not "think" much anymore into the depth of our faith. Some of us, then, stopped "wondering."

What we forgot or simply were never taught, however, is that the God whom the early century Christian

fathers, bishops, theologians, and even the writers of the
Christian scriptures envisioned was a God understood
within the context of *their* cosmology, their philosophy, their culture, and their worldview. Theirs was for
the most part the Hellenic worldview of the time, which
could accommodate only a God "out there" and "up
there," a God apart, dwelling in a definite place called
heaven. "He" was our almighty "Father," who sat on a
throne, to whom Jesus after his resurrection "ascended,"
and at whose right hand he now sits. We were taught that
we need to earn this God's favor, and that Jesus helped
us in this by sacrificing himself for us on the cross and
opening for us the gates of heaven that had been shut
to us because of Adam's sin. It was explained to us that
once we receive the grace that sanctifies us through the
suffering and death of Jesus, it is incumbent upon us that
we persevere in this state earned for us on the cross by
our Savior. In that way we would gain eternal salvation.

THE CHALLENGE

The question that my "dream student" asked me this
morning is centered around the disquiet he feels with
this kind of explanation of salvation. I felt that my challenge was to let him know somehow that God's presence
and influence in our life is much bigger than this story
allows and that if he and my other dream-students feel
uncomfortable with, or even uninterested in, this rendition of our salvation history, they are not alone.

Perception Shift

We live in an age of major perception shifts. The discoveries of science tell us today that concepts such as up and down, inside and outside, far and near, past and future are merely constructs of our way of seeing and therefore understanding the world around us. I have discussed the emerging worldview of our time in a number of my books,[29] as well as in the previous chapter and, therefore, do not wish to burden the reader by repeating myself, except to help focus our discussion. Suffice it to say therefore that, supported by the scientific discoveries of our time, we know a universe today that manifests total interconnectedness and relationality, infinite possibilities, and constant change. We know today, furthermore, that human expectations help create what human beings of any culture see and understand, that our reality therefore is malleable, if you will, and ever is related to us. Because of this knowledge, we realize that our world "gives itself to us" at this time in history differently from the way it did in Hellenic, medieval, or Renaissance times, and that our interpretations of it need to change. It is only reasonable to expect, therefore, that these changes must be verbalized in ways that can be understood by, and be meaningful to, contemporary Christians.

The youngsters growing up now are immersed in this new worldview, whether they are conscious of this or not, just as we until just recently were, in many respects unknowingly, immersed in the previous worldview. A

God above and outside is meaningless in the new perspective, because there really is no outside. The perennial experience of the mystic's silent openness and intimacy with the Divine as "mystery that is all-encompassing" speaks more readily to the religious consciousness of today than do clean definitions, declarations of certitudes, and eternal truths. The former "God above" manifests today as a "God within"—permeating and suffusing all, as the love energy that flows in and through everything, as the God William Blake spoke of in his prophetic *Jerusalem* vision cited earlier.

Strangely, and as if to illustrate what I have just written, I received a phone call from a friend of mine a short while ago. She told me that, in the last little while, she had been struggling to overcome "wounds from her childhood": in her case, what she perceived to be an inordinate need "to be special," to be recognized and loved. During her morning prayer today, while lying in bed with her hands folded over her heart, she had called out to God wondering about God's presence in her life. "I saw myself as a little girl," she said, "head bowed down and shoulders sunken in, crying and at the same time defensive—trying to protect myself from getting hurt. Suddenly, as I was watching myself that way and feeling abandoned, I received a most beautiful and totally unexpected gift. It came in the form of a simple message: *What you are looking for is already within you. You do not need to look outside yourself for the love you desire.*

Recognize it as already and always within you—flowing through you, pouring forth without diminishing. Let it pour out, and you will find inner peace."

Our God is a God within us and all around us. There is no distance between us and the Source of our being. We are enveloped by the Divine. God does not need to come "under our roof." We really do not stand or kneel *before* "Him," nor do we need to wonder about our unworthiness—a term, I believe, with which God is totally unfamiliar. One of my favorite mantras echoes Blake's *Jerusalem*: "I in You and You in me." It is a prayer of immanent presence and healing. To dwell in the recognition of this infinite tenderness is indeed grace, as Symeon, the New Theologian, whom I keep quoting wherever I go, recognized already in the tenth century:

> For if we genuinely love Him,
> we wake up inside Christ's body
> where all our body, all over,
> every most hidden part of it,
> is realized in joy as Him,
> and He makes us utterly, real,
> and everything that is hurt, everything
> that seemed to us dark, harsh, shameful,
> maimed, ugly, irreparably
> damaged, is in Him transformed
> and recognized as whole, as lovely,
> and radiant in His light
> we awaken as the Beloved
> in every last part of our body.

FOCUSING THE ISSUE

Would my "dream student" have understood all of the above? I want to believe he would have. This way of thinking and the attitude it engenders is ever more appropriate for today and affects all our previous interpretations of our sacred Story. As I mentioned in the previous chapter, sacrificial atonement for a sin passed on through our parents' sexual pleasure makes little sense today, particularly to young people. A God who demanded this of "His" Son appears cruel and vengeful, especially since the "sin" is never explained and, if referred back to Adam, seems even more inconceivable. In this regard, the renowned scripture scholar and founding member of the well-known Jesus Seminar, John Dominic Crossan, maintains that "Christian theology has not been as careful as is necessary with [its explanation of redemption via] vicarious atonement. It has converted a gift offered upward and graciously accepted by God into a demand coming downward and implacably demanded by God. But divinely *demanded* vicarious atonement is a theological obscenity."[30]

In homilies published late in his life, Sebastian Moore calls the atonement theory "the big religious mistake about God." He begins *Saving Passion,* a sermon on this topic as follows:

> As we again inch up to the crucial event of all history, I feel the need further to exorcise a notion that has absolutely bedevilled our thinking about

the sacrifice of Calvary. This is the pestilential notion, never spelt out because it can't be without blasphemy, that Calvary is a human sacrifice in the primitive sense that, because of the theological status of the victim, is acceptable to God. This never-spelt-out idea tries to preserve itself like a neurosis, for it suits precisely the cruelty in the psyche that God is working to cure us of.[31]

Moore suggests that it might come "as a shock suddenly to realize that God did not want sacrifice" and that "Christ's passion was precisely the end of such bloody rituals [in order] to change humanity for ever."[32]

The shock can, of course, be pleasant or frightening, depending on how much thought one has given to the theory of redemption and how attached one is to idols three and four. Here the words of Tad W. Guzie, S.J., might be reassuring. He tells us:

Important facts are *always* interpreted. . . . Once we get used to interpretations of an event, it is not at all easy to remember that *the event and the interpretation are not the same thing.* The one cannot simply be identified with the other. Interpretation begins as an effort to unfold the meaning of an event. But as the process of interpretation continues, it is not always controlled. Like a stone wrapped in a snowball and sent rolling down a snow-covered bank, the event can get so wrapped in interpretations, one layer

added to another, that there is sometimes little
relationship between the last layer and the first
fact lying somewhere inside.[33]

When one interpretation, therefore, gets identified as
the only true one and is claimed to be infallibly so, fear
can shock us into rejecting any other way of seeing the
event, and guilt can prevent us from thinking for ourselves according to the context of our time. We discussed
this dilemma of Catholic thought in a previous chapter
and can only be grateful for those theologians who see
their task as ongoing and allow themselves some tentativeness as they journey ever more deeply into what they
have truly encountered as Mystery.

In her well known study of early Christianity (*In
Memory of Her*), Elisabeth Schüssler Fiorenza reas-
sures us that our earliest Christian ancestors avoided the
notion of sacrificial atonement. The notion of sacrifice
was eschewed by the earliest Jesus tradition, she says,
which did not see "the ministry and death of Jesus in
cultic terms as atonement for sins."[34] Along with the German scholar Hans Kessler, she maintains that this "concept originated among Christians who not only spoke
Greek but were also thoroughly at home in the Greek-
Hellenistic thought world."[35]

There were a number of reasons, during the first
century and beyond, for the eventual development of a
sacrificial dimension to the death of Jesus and ultimately
to the celebration of the Eucharist in memory of him.

Nevertheless, we can be assured, as the German scholar Herbert Haag points out:

> The conviction that God had no need of sacrifices was firmly rooted in early Christianity. Following Jesus' example it radically rejected the bloody sacrifices of the temple and in doing so had a special liking for using Old Testament texts hostile to ritual [the Psalms, as well as Amos 5:21–22; 5:24; 5:25, and Hosea 6:6]. The same aversion [was] also . . . directed against all pagan examples of sacrifice, something which . . . brought Christians into conflict with the Roman State.[36]

The factual event of some two thousand years ago was that Jesus of Nazareth was crucified by the Romans. Because of who he was and what he had preached, his death and the events that followed were *interpreted* over the years. His sacrificial death in cultic terms as atonement for our sins was *one* interpretation. A legitimate question for today, then, is whether there can be other noncultic and valid interpretations.

CULTURAL INFLUENCES AT THE TIME

The Roman state was not god-less or unbelieving. In fact Romans strongly maintained that their deities required and deserved respect, honor, and propitiation through sacrifice. Proper ritual worship was seen, therefore, as necessary to maintain their gods' favor and continued support for the empire. A meal, even if a religious meal such as Christians celebrated, was not seen as satisfying this necessity, and Christians were, therefore, regarded with suspicion and hostility. Although they defended their position that "true worship is that of the heart and of love," early Christians in the Greco-Roman world soon felt themselves pressured "to ascribe a sacrificial character to the simple eucharistic meal,"[37] and so it eventually was proclaimed as an "unbloody sacrifice" offered in union with Christ's self-offering to God on Calvary for the forgiveness of our sins.

With cultic sacrifice, the need for "priesthood" also became inevitable but was not fully claimed until the third century. "In the whole Christian literature of the first two centuries the term *hiereus, sacerdos*, 'priest,' is avoided."[38] It was foreign to the early Christians even to expect the "overseers" (*episkopoi*) and "servants" (*diakonoi*) to exercise "sacred offices or ministries or indeed forming a hierarchy, or priestly order."[39] Only by the end of the second century, notably with the letters of Ignatius of Antioch, do we see "the earliest evidence for the monarchical episcopate and the hierarchy of bishop (always in the singular), *presbyterium*, and deacons"—a vision pointing to what is now so familiar to us.[40]

My purpose for discussing the issue of "priesthood" and its original Christian connection with our sacred meal-turned-into -"sacrifice" was to offer a possible reason for the shock or surprise that some may experience when what has long been presented as "originating" with Jesus himself and with the twelve apostles, as well as what we have come to understand as "salvation through atonement," are given their historical context, and shown as *interpretations* of an event, not necessarily as *the event* itself. It seems clear to me that the respectful reconsideration of our understanding of salvation beyond obligatory crucifixion demanded by an offended deity is necessary for our times and their context. This task is being undertaken by numerous religious thinkers of today so that, as adult Christians, we might truly accept our personal and God-given role in our salvation.

6

WHAT ABOUT SALVATION?

Jesus's passion for the kingdom of God led to what is often called his passion, namely, his suffering and death. But to restrict Jesus' passion to his suffering and death is to ignore the passion that brought him to Jerusalem. To think of Jesus' passion as simply what happened on Good Friday is to separate his death from the passion that animated his life.

—Marcus J. Borg and John Dominic Crossan

The questions that open up for us in the light of the above reflections, therefore, will need to focus on a more meaningful interpretation of Jesus as our Savior, as well as on a different and hopefully deeper understanding of sin and the alienation we experience because of it. As I mentioned already, it is a historical fact that Jesus of Nazareth was crucified by the Romans. Our scriptures tell us that he was handed over by the high priests of his own faith. The execution, therefore, was perpetrated both by the "powers of domination" presiding over his religion, and by the imperial power of Rome in control of the Jewish people at that time.

Scripture scholars generally connect the reason for his execution to his message. The peace of Rome (*Pax Romana*) was achieved through total domination, war, and violence; the peace Jesus proclaimed was, even to the end, through nonviolence:

> "Love your enemy."
> "Do good to those who hate you."
> "Forgive seventy times seven times."
> "Father, forgive them for they know not
>   what they do."

These are sayings we all know well. We also know that the society that Jesus envisioned and modeled by his life was "brokerless," as John Dominic Crossan calls it. Jesus assured us that no mediation was necessary between God and us. He did not see himself as mediator but rather showed us the "way," modeling access to the Divine, and inviting all of us—sinner or saint, gentile or Jew, slave or free, woman or man, poor or rich—to embrace it: "When you pray say: Father," he taught us, *not*: "Father of Jesus who art in heaven." He preached, healed, exorcised, but claimed no special status, except that of teacher. He knew he was the child of God and wanted all of us to claim that relationship as well.

THE DOMINATION SYSTEM

If Jesus had one enemy, it was the system of domination and oppression that was pervasive in his time and continues to be so today—in spite of our claim on him and on his vision for close to two thousand years.

Walter Wink, in his magnificent study of Jesus, *The Human Being: Jesus and the Enigma of the Son of the Man,* singles out Jesus' critique of the domination system as "the most radical and comprehensive framework for understanding what he was about." He claims that it provides "the primary criterion for discerning what was *revelatory* in Jesus' life and message."[41] In *From Religion Back to Faith* I have already discussed how Wink identifies the Domination System as pervasive in Jesus' time, as well as in ours.[42] Let me here simply point out that the continued oppression of women and children by patriarchy, economic exploitation, oppressive roles imposed on children through socialization, hierarchical and self-serving power arrangements so prevalent in his time and in ours, claims of racial superiority, the subversion of the law to the advantage of the powerful, rules of purity that segregate people, and finally, as we already discussed, the entire sacrificial system advocating sacred violence—all are death-dealing examples of this system.

The extensive research and writings of both John Dominic Crossan and Markus Borg amply substantiate this claim. In their mutual study, dealing with the last week before the crucifixion and death of Jesus, they describe his public resistance to the injustices and domination of his time and identify this as the main reason for his execution.

> As Mark tells the story, was Jesus guilty of non-violent resistance to imperial Roman oppression and local Jewish collaboration? Oh, yes. Mark's story of Jesus' final week is a sequence of public demonstrations against and confrontations with the domination system. And, as all know, it killed him.[43]

They also see our rejection of, and stance against, this kind of oppression as central to, and in fact, as *the* test of, discipleship:[44]

> You know that among the rulers of the Gentiles those whom they recognize as their rulers lord it over them, and their great ones are tyrants over them. But it is not so among you; but whoever wishes to become great among you must be your servant, and whoever wishes to be first among you must be slave of all. (Mark 10:42–44)

Borg, in his own extensive work on Jesus, cites Jesus' vision as "God's passion for the earth," God's dream, God's will that humans should live under divine rule and experience a state (mode of life) or social climate signaling "the end of injustice and violence, [where] everybody will have enough, and nations will not make war on nations anymore."[45]

THE VISION OF JESUS

No reference to the "heavenly hereafter" is implied by this vision, however. I am referring here to the frequent misinterpretation that praises misery now and sees heaven as a reward for suffering. The vision of Jesus was for this world. The view that emerged in later years, claiming a world where suffering is sanctioned by God or even sent by God to those "He" loves—assuring them a greater or superior reward in heaven—is simply unsubstantiated in the life of Jesus. This does, of course, not mean that, given the domination system, there will not be suffering and the persecution of those who stand for justice. God blesses them, however, for their uncompromised righteousness in the face of suffering, not for their suffering in and of itself, which was most certainly not willed by God.

The follower of Jesus works for justice, for a world where everybody has a right to God's bounty and can achieve a wholesome, healthy, and happy life. The follower of Jesus works for and embraces a community where everyone is allowed to think and express thought, to love and express love according to his or her reality, where everyone is welcome at the banquet table: the publicans and sinners of today, the nobodies, the undesirables, the beggars and prostitutes, the alien and outcast, the rich and the poor.

A church that defends domination, "princedoms," the subjugation of women or of anyone who disagrees with the prevailing "power opinion" as the will of God, betrays and subverts this vision. Jesus rejected exclusion, oppression, and self-aggrandizement in his day. He rejects it in our day as well. He was killed because he challenged those who claimed the status of domination and used it against him. *That* was the sin of his time and in his world, from which he wanted to save, to free, his people—the Jewish people and all those suffering from oppression. *That* is the sin of our time and in our world also, from which his message is meant to save us still. To this day domination wages war against freedom and love. At times it openly rejects the message of Jesus; at other times it shamelessly claims to stand with him. It has done so in its wars, crusades, and inquisitions. It continues to do so through policies of oppression, exclusion, silencing, investigations, and excommunications without recourse. Jesus, as our Savior, shared with us the vision of Mark 10:42–44. He was executed because of his openly expressed and lived convictions, but we believe that God vindicated him, hailed him as God's own, and that in *that* vindication his message as God's will is confirmed.

The early followers of Jesus also proclaimed his vision. Assuming for Jesus the titles usually reserved for

Caesar, they hailed him as the Son of God, their leader and "Lord." "Jesus is of God," they claimed, implying that Caesar and Caesar's dominion had no power over them. They lived and they died for this vision, which they saw as their salvation. They could do this because of their resurrection experience, which had affirmed everything he had said and done, and highlighted his death as that of a servant of God murdered by cruel and power-hungry humanity. Sebastian Moore tells us in a tender and very credible way how God "interprets" the crucifixion of Jesus and his vindication. He has God say to us:

> Folks, let's call things by their names. It's murder. You did my boy in, and it's by forgiving you this most deeply rooted sin that I change you forever. So let's have a party to celebrate till the end of the world your emancipation from hating me and killing one another to disguise this ugly secret.[46]

There is no mention here of atonement. We hear, instead, a loving and all-merciful God inviting humankind into the Gospel vision of Jesus.

The scripture parallel for this kind of God is, of course, the story of the "prodigal" and utterly generous father who does not desire restitution and apologies from his renegade, spendthrift son, but throws a party to celebrate forgiveness and reconciliation before an apology or atonement is even offered. Salvation, I believe, is in the celebration of this Gospel vision that emancipates us from the need for restitution and atonement into unconditional forgiveness. It liberates us from an image of God who exacts a penance for every wrong done, sends us suffering when we do evil (or simply to tempt us), and rewards us for the good we do. The vision of Jesus offers us the healing power of love and *only that*.

Here, finally, we find the answer to my "dream student's" question. Our salvation is found in a *way of life* that calls for imitation and presents a Christian vision for the here and now. Its emphasis is not primarily on the next world, nor on events of salvation extraneous to us. Why the Nicene as well as Apostles' Creed skip this most essential message of our faith modeled by the life of Jesus has always puzzled me. They both go immediately from his birth to his suffering and death and skip his life, message, and ministry all together. Yet in our following of him, his life is primary. Our journey into God is not a passive affair—something that is done for us, or was completed some two thousand years ago. We are his Body and as such are intimately involved in the event of Christification now.

CONCLUSION

Perhaps no scripture story points more convincingly to the still prevailing interpretation of the crucifixion of Jesus than the story of his agony in the garden of Gethsemane. Has this story not been interpreted through the ages as the struggle of Jesus with his impending death and his plea to God that the "cup" might pass—that the

"Father," somehow might change the demand made of him as "God-man" to repay the debt incurred by Adam (the head of humanity) against God? We are told that he expressed his submission to the will of God in this regard, and that God sent an angel (mentioned only in Luke) to reassure him, but did not take away the demand for restitution.

What puzzles me in this story is that scripture provides no witnesses to this event; the disciples were sleeping. One could easily ask, therefore, who it was that heard Jesus' plea and saw the angel. Jesus was alone. In the light of this, I wonder whether, in order to make it meaningful for us today, an attempt at reimagining or reinterpreting this event (that nobody witnessed) might not be helpful. Could we perhaps move it beyond the insulting notion that God demanded restitution and wanted the crucifixion? Could we allow ourselves to be invited into this moment—as partakers, not merely as listeners to a past event recounted for our edification?

In order to do this, the emphasis needs to be placed, once again, on Jesus—the man. We remember his integrity and his consistent stand against domination and oppression. We can surmise, therefore, that he knew what he had done that week in Jerusalem.[47] He had confronted the oppressors, the "brokers" of God's favor, especially in the Temple. He had cleansed it (symbolically destroyed it), and protested its sacrificial emphasis and stress on mediation. He had preached against

hypocrisy and falsehood, and more than once the "powers" had wanted to arrest him but could not "for fear of
the crowd" that followed him.

Jesus was a man—young, but not naïve. He knew
that he was in danger from those who hated him. He was
aware of the malcontent among his followers and the
danger of betrayal. He knew that any denunciation by
the high priests, appointed by Rome to keep the people
subdued, would quickly lead to his death. He knew they
rejected him and his message and were only looking for
an opportunity to hand him over to the Romans. The
road outside Jerusalem was lined with crosses that witnessed to swift executions—no questions asked. Pilate,
we are told by modern exegetes, was not a friendly man.
He was cruel and monstrous, in fact, and sentences of
execution were frequent.[48] In the light of this, I want to
believe that on that night in the garden, facing imminent danger, Jesus struggled with himself. He was young
and had a mission that had barely begun. His followers
needed more help to understand his vision. They had
not shown signs of really comprehending all that was
involved in witnessing to the reign of God. Even now,
when he needed their support, they were sleeping. Jesus
felt alone and afraid.

There were of course options, and Jesus would have
known that. He could flee. Bethany was close, though
outside the city, which Jews usually did not leave during Passover. He had friends there who could hide him.

He could also hide in the caves of the garden. He could back down and retract when confronted—a modern option not really open to a man such as he. I believe he struggled with these options and with the knowledge that if he took them, the message would be betrayed and he would betray himself as well. I see this kind of struggle as the profoundest kind of obedience, the deepest discernment, since it involves the mature person before God— with the values she or he has espoused, the society that challenges them, and his or her own very real temptation to avoid suffering. I believe that Jesus struggled and prayed that night for guidance, and that he received an answer from deep within himself. It did not come in the form of an order from above, but rather from his uncompromised connection to a loving Parent-God.

When I listen to this story in my heart, this is what I hear God tell Jesus:

> *"Dearest One, I do not want you to die either. I hate coercion and suffering, torture and crucifixion. I do not want any of these for anyone at any time, and definitely not for you, my Beloved. **But there are, as you well know, some things more important than life**. There is your own integrity and the integrity of the message. If you run, it will be easy to disclaim the message: "He is no different from anyone else," they will say. "When the going gets rough, he leaves us and runs." And they will go back to their discouragement and cyni-*

*cism and lost-ness from which you were called to
save them.*

Jesus, I believe, heard this response from God in the
depth of his heart, and so he did not flee; he stayed. He
stood before his enemies and executioners, defied violence, spoke when he needed to, and otherwise chose
the path of silence. They crucified him. *God raised him,
and he lives still.* That, I believe, is our story—a story relevant for us today. I am convinced that Dorothy Stang, the
martyr of Brazil, heard that message from God as well.
She had a way out. She could have stayed in the United
States. She chose to return, in spite of death threats. She
did so, because *there are some things more important
than life.* Archbishop Romero heard that message also,
as did the six Jesuit and four women martyrs of El Sal-
vador, the Sister Adorers of the Blood of Christ in Libe-
ria, and men and women throughout the ages who have
stood against oppression and witnessed to the vision of
Jesus. They suffered and died, not for the sake of suffering, nor in atonement to an angry God, but because *there
are some things more important than life.*

The greatness of Christianity lies primarily in its
members, in its martyrs, its teachers, its visionaries:
Those heroic ones known (or never recognized) who
were grasped by its vision and lived it. The greatness
of Christianity lies in the phoenix-like effect their lives,
their deaths, their sufferings, their courage in the face
of oppression had on the world and has on each one of

us still. Domination, patriarchal cruelty, and oppression do not make greatness and save no one. They can just as easily foster counter oppression, hate, cowardice, and betrayal. We can safely say, therefore, that the betrayal and crucifixion of Jesus were not justified by his resurrection. *His life and his teaching, his vision and the courage with which he proclaimed it were.* God vindicated him because he stood for God's reign, and nothing could force him to betray it. Crucifixion is evil and can never be justified. It is no different from hangings, beheadings, shootings, the electric chair, lethal injections, and the guillotine. God wills none of these—not for the just, nor for the unjust. God blesses martyrs through the ages for their work in bringing about God's reign, for their witness and their courage even in the face of persecution. God's dream is that their witness will change the world into a place where torture is no longer usedsee and domination gives way to mutuality and love. Any religion, therefore, that attributes any kind of violence to God, or sees it willed by God, is not worthy of its name.

The validation of Christianity lies in the resurrection—the vindication of the Just One and his message. Our faith holds its power through this vindication and the transformation toward justice it continues to inspire. It betrays its power by forgetting or neglecting the message and the vision. The critical question of salvation through Christ, therefore, is answered only in terms of transformation. Its criterion is never in terms of how much one has suffered, but always in terms of how the world has evolved toward greater love.

Biologist Rupert Sheldrake has popularized for us the theory of morphic resonance, which opens up once again the question of whether the world is indeed a better place because of Christianity. Sheldrake's theory holds that when a member of a species changes behavior that is then imitated by fellow members, eventually a critical mass is reached, which brings about the behavioral change in the entire species. It would seem to me that the number of Christians in the world has certainly reached the critical mass in terms of the entire human race. The painful question, however, persists: Is the world a better place—more peace-filled, hospitable, generous, inclusive, accepting of diversity, loving, less violent, arrogant, divisive, greedy, power hungry—because of Christianity? That after all was what Jesus modeled for our living. Perhaps it would be more helpful for us, but also more challenging, to make the question more personal: Is the world a better place because I believe in the vision of Jesus Christ? And if that is too overwhelming: Is my country, my city, my neighborhood, my parish, my family more wholesome, healthier, happier because of me and my commitment to the vision of Jesus?

7

ON BEING HIS BODY

You were right before me
But I had moved away from myself.
I could not find myself.
How much less, then, could I find you.
—St. Augustine (*Confessions*)

A number of years ago in Los Angeles, where I had been asked to give some workshops at the Religious Education Conference, I was awakened early in the morning of one of my lecture days by the music and lyrics of one of our Eucharistic acclamations reverberating in my head. The text is an adaptation taken from Paul's first letter to the Corinthians 11:26: "For as often as you eat this bread and drink the cup, you proclaim Christ's death until Christ comes." The musical rendition of the Eucharistic acclamation (before the 2011 liturgical changes) has us affirm what Paul says: "When we eat this bread and drink this cup, we proclaim your death, Lord Jesus, until you come in glory." The melody and words "sang" themselves first, I suppose, in my unconscious and then moved me into consciousness, repeating themselves, as melodies can, over and over again until I began to wonder what they were meant to tell me.

My thoughts centered on the "death" that we affirm as we break bread and share the cup, and I wondered what it signifies for us today. After all, during the liturgical celebration we proclaim his death in the face of his living presence among us who are called together in love. Why? It came to me, as I pondered this, that perhaps it is not the event on Calvary, as such, that we are primarily professing, but rather *our* dying in solidarity, a dying *with* him to which we commit ourselves when we make this proclamation. He died for the sake of love, for a world fashioned according to God's plan, a world of compassion, of peace and mutual acceptance. Perhaps the dying we proclaim is our dying to everything in us that prevents such a world from coming into existence. At every Eucharist we are, in fact, acknowledging our membership as his Body, offering ourselves as one with him—to be "re-membered" into his Body, to live for, and be part of, the vision. Perhaps the proclamation does not refer merely to something done some two thousand years ago and simply recalled during our Eucharistic celebration, something in the past, and now merely witnessed by us as it is being offered once again for us by the priest at the altar; something that renders us passive recipients only. Perhaps, instead, it is happening in, and depends on, every member of the assembly gathered in prayer and involved in the redemptive act that is ever in the process of "Christification."

Could not the death that we proclaim as a precursor to Christ's coming in glory mean *our* death to self-absorption, for example, to intransigence, to greed, divisiveness and exclusiveness, to violence and war, to our rejection of, and indifference to, each other and especially to the weak and vulnerable, the outcasts of our culture? Might it not mean our intentional rejection of the domination system that Jesus denounced in word and deed, and that ultimately killed him? If the death proclaimed by us means all that, and we, as the living members of his Body, consciously accept responsibility for that; if as church, we dedicate ourselves to this death and get actively involved with spreading the compassion of God, would not Christ be coming in glory at this very moment? There would be no need to wait for the Parousia. The reign of God would be well on the way.

I cannot help thinking that this is what Paul meant by his reference to the Eucharistic meal as a proclamation of "Christ's death until Christ comes." It is interesting to note that Paul's first letter to the Corinthians, mentioned above as the source of our Eucharistic acclamation, was in fact not a happy missive. Paul was very upset with the church of Corinth and reprimanded them for their lack of compassion, for their selfishness, for their divisiveness, and for their lack of sincerity. He chastised them for their indifference to the poor among them: "For when the time comes to eat, each of you goes ahead with your own supper, and one goes hungry and another becomes drunk. What! Do you not have homes to eat and drink in? Or do you show contempt for the church of God and humiliate those who have nothing?" (11:20–22). This passage is immediately followed by Paul's reminding the Corinthians of the Lord's Supper and the proclamation of a new covenant—a *different vision.*

The statement we have meditated on above challenges them to take seriously their membership in this vision. It seems that they remembered the glory of the resurrection by which they saw their religion justified but ignored the poor among them. They did not reflect on what belonging to Christ Jesus implied, and what was asked of them. They came and ate the consecrated bread at some time during their gathering. They shared the cup. They did their duty, but they had forgotten that Christianity above all is *experiential,* an action-oriented religion, and that pro-forma presence without regard for the other members present with them means nothing. "Whatsoever you do to the least . . . you do to me" (Matt. 25:40). Paul concludes his letter with a stern warning of which the following observation strikes me as particularly important: "For all who eat and drink without discerning the body, eat and drink judgment against themselves" (11:29).

BE WHAT YOU SEE;
BECOME WHAT YOU ARE

St. Augustine follows this Pauline perspective in his admonition that when we receive Christ's Body, we "Be what [we] see; become what [we] are." For the well-known sacramental theologian Regis Duffy, this means that "our symbols and the praxis of our lives cannot be separated."[49] I have cited Augustine's more detailed advice in *Awe-Filled Wonder,* but it bears repeating:

> If you want to know what is the Body of Christ, hear what the Apostle tells believers: "You are Christ's Body and his members" (1 Cor. 12:27). If, then, you are Christ's Body and his members, it is your symbol that lies on the Lord's altar— what you receive is a symbol of yourself. When you say "Amen" to what you are, your saying it affirms it. You hear [the priest say] "The Body of Christ," and you answer "Amen," and you must be the Body of Christ to make that "Amen" take effect.   — St. Augustine (Sermon 272)

At times I do wonder whether our Christian culture today is really that different from the one at Corinth. Are we in our daily lives any less selfish, any more aware of the poor among us? How ready are we today to live Eucharistic lives? I am thinking, for example, of our entitlement programs for which all of us are asked to pay. Are they not frequently interpreted as privileges that a nation "begrudgingly" grants to those who are elderly or poor, favors that those who "have" inconvenience themselves through taxation to bestow on those who "have not"?

I wonder what Paul would say to us? Is our Eucharistic meal, are the other sacraments as well, transformative for our lives and our values, or are they obligatory routine dimensions of our lives, "performed" for us by the presbyterate, and reducing us to passive recipients with few or no concerns other than attendance? Is ours an "underdeveloped and undercontextualized" participation, as Regis Duffy suggests? Is what he questioned in 1982 still true today? Could it be, for example, that some of us stress "the 'real presence' of Christ in the Eucharist . . . to avoid dealing with the lack of real presence in a crowded church on Sunday morning?"[50] The answer Duffy gives to the problem in Corinth, which he identifies as "so much sacrament and so little commitment," is simply: "Worship and sacrament that cost the user little."[51] Is this true for us?

I ended the last chapter by referring to questions I am in the habit of asking students or participants in my workshops at the beginning of our time together. I use them to help us take responsibility for the Christian vision we espouse: Is the world a better place because of Christianity? And more personally even: Is the world a better place because I am a Christian? These are daring questions that cannot be answered glibly in the affirmative. The transformation Jesus preached and modeled is at stake here, and it is ours, as his Body, to bring about. Jesus called us to inner conversion on that night before he died when he broke bread, shared the cup, and proclaimed a new covenant. He spoke of a covenant that he had already lived and proclaimed every time he had broken and shared bread throughout his public life. His open table fellowship and free healing had earned him the title of glutton and drunkard among his enemies. He was known as a friend of tax collectors and sinners (Luke 7:34). He spoke to women publicly, healed them, and included them among his followers. He invited himself and his followers into the houses of outcasts (Jews who acted like gentiles) and ate with them. He forgave his crucifiers and promised a dying thief that he would share paradise with him that very day.

The conversion to commensality, to open and inclusive table fellowship and a community of free healing that allows for this, however difficult it may be, *that* is the "haunt of grace" that will not leave us alone. It is the Spirit of God, the "Hound of Heaven," who pursues us and ever calls us to "become what we are": the Body of Christ here on earth, his living presence. So when we make the Eucharistic acclamation proclaiming his death until he comes in glory, the "coming" and the "glory" are really about his coming *in us*, once we say "yes" to the death, over and over again; his coming *in us*, as we see and recognize his presence and his power and his love, and accept these into our lives as ours to share.

All this clearly involves a new way of seeing or, we might call it, a "rejuvenated" way of seeing that returns us to the Source, to the One who wanted us to have a symbol—a gathering point—for our at-oneness in him. We could perhaps say, then, that Eucharist is in fact much bigger than "transubstantiation" as such, though it does not do away with presence. Eucharist is more than the effect of the words of institution uttered by one man for the assembly. *Eucharist is the event of the community gathered in remembrance of their covenant in Christ to be about the reign of God.* It is the presencing that happens when the Body commits itself ever again to be about what Jesus the Christ called them to on that last night before he died; what he called them to throughout his life, namely, the justice agenda of God's reign symbolized in the washing of the feet.

> *Do you know what I have done to you? You call me Teacher and Lord—and you are right, for that is what I am. So if I, your Lord and Teacher, have washed your feet, you also ought to wash one another's feet.* (John 13:12–14)

Eucharist is the feast of "foot washers." It happens in love and in the remembering of Him who set us the example. Michael Himes said it so well when he paraphrased the words of Jesus: "Where two or three are gathered in love, *I am what happens between them.*"[52]

Instead of doing away with real presence, therefore, we broaden it and lay less stress on the power of the words spoken, and more stress on the commitment of the assembly, presided over by their leader, to *be* the Body, and "presence" that Body in the actual events of love shared and justice happening among us. When we gather in love, Christ is present in our midst under the appearance of bread and wine. It is clear that in order to think these musings with equanimity, we need to be able to allow our thinking to expand rather than contract. It is not that we reject tradition; we simply allow it to embrace more of what today we know Jesus was about.

For those who feel a certain dis-ease at our attempt to see greater communal involvement in the Eucharistic event than we normally understand and have generally been taught, it may be of interest to realize that few of our beliefs, if any, were ironclad at the beginning of Christianity. Eucharistic presence was in a process of development for quite a long time. The belief in transubstantiation, for example, became part of our understanding of the Eucharist only somewhere at the end of the first millennium in the documents of the Magisterium. It was further developed and formally used only around 1130 C.E as a way of underlining the objectivity of the change in the Eucharistic bread and wine. The Fourth Lateran Council officially declared it in 1215 C.E., and later in that century it was more fully developed in the theology of Thomas Aquinas (1225–74). The reliance on Aristotelian philosophy is clear in Thomas and distances the dogma significantly from the early Christian meal and open table fellowship.

Real presence in physical form was one of the major dividing points between Ambrosian and Augustinian traditions in the first half of the first millennium. Ambrose emphasized the changing of the bread and wine into

Christ's body and blood, although he did not say how
this change occurred. Augustine, as Mary T. Malone
indicates and as we already noted earlier in the citation
of one of his sermons, "stressed the dynamic symbolic
unifying power of the sacrament, incorporating all into
the mystical body of Christ."[53] The debate continued
into the thirteenth century and finally did away with the
earlier and, in my view, deeply empowering notion "of
the eucharistic as spiritual refreshment and the bread
of heaven, as a pledge of the church's unity and the one
unbroken body of Christ."[54]

The relationship to God that Jesus modeled for us
throughout his public ministry is one of *love in action.*
His was not primarily, if at all, a system of thought. *"Do
this in memory of me"* was his request, *not,* "Think this,
explain this, in memory of me. Learn what it means and
dogmatize it so everyone can get it right." Our intense
preoccupation with categories of understanding was,
as we discussed in chapter 3, a later development due
to Christianity's enculturation into a Greco-Roman culture. I want to believe that Jesus was (and continues to
be *through us* who are his Body) a social transformer,
a visionary of what can be, a revolutionary who non-
violently worked at opening minds and hearts toward
a world of compassion, mutuality, and justice. This
is as necessary in our time as it was in his. When we
claim him as our "Lord," therefore, we claim his path,
his values, his nonviolence, his inclusion and compassion. We take on his Body as ours and are transformed

— "transubstantiated" in him—a sacramental people whose life is holy—centered in God, and whose sacred symbols celebrate this holiness.

Eucharist

He was old, tired , and sweaty, pushing his home-made cart down the alley, stopping now and then to poke around in somebody's garbage. I wanted to tell him about eucharist but the look in his eyes, the despair in his face, the hopelessness of some-body else's life in his cart told me to forget it. So I smiled and said "Hi"... and gave him eucharist.

She was cute, nice build, too much paint, a little wobbly on her feet as she slid from her bar stool, and definitely on the make. "No thanks, not tonight"... and I gave her eucharist.

She lived alone, her husband dead, her family gone, and she talked at you, not to you. Words, endless words, spilled out. So I listened . . . and gave her eucharist. . . .

I laughed at myself, and said, "you with all your pains and selfishness, I forgive you, I accept you, I love you." It's nice and so necessary too . . . to give yourself eucharist.

Tired, weary, disgusted, lonely, go to your friends, open the door, say, "Look at me"... and receive their eucharist.

[Holy One] when will we learn, you cannot talk eucharist, cannot philosophize about it . . . you do it.

You don't dogmatize eucharist, sometimes you laugh it, sometimes you cry it. Often you sing it. Sometimes it's wild peace, then dying hurt, often humiliating, never deserved. You see eucharist in another's eyes, give it in another's hand to hold tight, squeeze it with an embrace. You pause, and eucharist with a million things to do—and a person who wants to talk, for eucharist is as simple as being on time, as profound as sympathy.

> *I give you my supper.*
> *I give you my sustenance.*
> *I give you my life.*
> *I give you me.*
> *I give you eucharist.*
>   —Author Unkown

This gentle reflection found its way onto my computer screen one day several years ago. I have no idea who sent it to me or who wrote it, but as I mentioned earlier, teachers today are found in the most surprising places, gracing us with unexpected depth. Deep down inside, we know that what they say rings true. Often it reaches far beyond the complexities of our dogmatic formulations and moves straight into our hearts.

· THOUGHTS AND QUESTIONS
FOR MEDITATION

1. "What we celebrate in Christ's birth is indeed the *core* of our Christian faith. Is not all of Christianity primarily about God birthing God's self into our very midst?". . . In Jesus of Nazareth— a human being very much like us, *what already was reached a climax.*" How do you understand this statement?

2. Even though our belief in the divinity of Jesus is important, why is it important for us to focus on the humanity of Jesus?

3. In the light of what you have been reading, how have you come to see the magnitude of the Incarnation?

4. How has the new worldview changed your view of God and your relationship to God? How would you answer the question of my "dream student" about Jesus as our savior?

5. Is the shock Sebastian Moore talks about regarding the change in the salvation narrative pleasant or frightening for you? Or is there no shock at all?

6. If you agree with Tad W. Guzie's statement that "important facts are *always* interpreted," what does this say to you about facts?

7. What are your thoughts about the origin of priesthood as discussed in these pages?

8. How have you experienced the "domination system"? Is it still real in our society and in our church?

9. How have you come to understand your own faith journey and the importance of Jesus in your life?

10. Who is the God of Jesus?

11. What is your reaction to the story of Christ's struggle in the garden before he was arrested, as depicted in these pages?

12. "The greatness of Christianity lies primarily in its members, in its martyrs, its teachers, its visionaries: those heroic ones known (or never recognized) who were grasped by its vision and lived it. The greatness of Christianity lies in the phoenix-like effect their lives, their deaths, their sufferings, their courage in the face of oppression had on the world and has on each one of us still." Is this true? Comment.

13. "Crucifixion is evil and can never be justified. It is no different from hangings, beheadings, shootings, the electric chair, lethal injections, and the guillotine. God wills none of these—not for the just, nor for the unjust." Do you agree?

14. "The painful question persists: Is the world a better place—more peace-filled, hospitable, generous,

inclusive, accepting of diversity, loving; less violent, arrogant, divisive, greedy, power hungry—because of Christianity? That after all was what Jesus modeled for our living." More directly: "Is my country, my city, my neighborhood, my parish, my family more wholesome, healthier, happier because of me and my commitment to the vision of Jesus?

15. Chapter 7 addresses the question of Christ's death proclaimed by us during the Eucharistic acclamation. How have you come to see it as moving us beyond the historical crucifixion of Jesus and including us as his Body? What, then, is his glory?

16. What has "being his Body" come to mean to you, concretely?

17. How have you come to understand what happens at the Eucharist?

Part IV

WHO DO YOU SAY I AM?

Chapter 8
The Cosmic Christ

Chapter 9
On Becoming Who We Are:
Divinity Unfolding

Chapter 10
Approaching the Mystery

8

THE COSMIC CHRIST

IT BEGAN
WITH AN ENCOUNTER

It began with an encounter. Some people—Aramaic- and perhaps also Greek-speaking Jews—came into contact with Jesus of Nazareth and stayed with him. This encounter, and what took place in the life of Jesus and in connection with his death, gave their personal lives new meaning and new significance. They felt that they had been born again, that they had been understood, and this new identity found expression in a similar solidarity towards others, their fellow-[human beings]. This change in the course of their lives was the result of their encounter with Jesus, for without him they would have remained what they had been (see 1 Cor. 15:17). It had not come about through any initiative of their own; it had simply happened to them.

—Edward Schillebeeckx

With these words Edward Schillebeeckx introduces his momentous study *Christ, The Experience of Jesus as Lord* —a sequel to his equally expansive work *Jesus, an Experiment in Christology.* I cannot remember any other scholarly reflection on Jesus the Christ that has moved me more profoundly than this simple observation at the beginning of Schillebeeckx's book, fittingly introduced with the title "Jesus, the story of a new lifestyle."

For this great scholar of the twentieth century, then, the momentous event called Christianity "began with an encounter." Simple words that carry enormous energy, largely because deep down all of us must admit that anything truly significant and life-changing in human existence always begins that way. Martin Buber called it the "I–thou" experience without which our humanity cannot flourish, since it alone helps us to glimpse eternity.[55] I believe that Jesus of Nazareth empowered his followers two thousand years ago and empowers us today to do precisely that—to glimpse eternity. He was an extraordinary human being whose *Thou* has permeated history, "who sparked, and through the ages has continued to spark, the fire of our yearning for authenticity, and human integrity."[56] Because of who he was, those who truly encountered him wanted to stay with him and in so doing their lives were changed: *Rabbi, where do you dwell? Come and see* (John 1:38–39).

We believe that Jesus embodied within himself the fullness of our humanity. We also believe that "it is no less than God with whom we are confronted in Jesus."[57] For me, this means that Jesus, as we have come to see him through the ages, manifested in his humanity the divine energy that courses through the universe and is waiting to be expressed and to become consciously acknowledged in all of us.

Today, when scientists touch the Mystery—that which defies all scientific formulations and invites them to move beyond the scientific realm—they refer to it by various names: "An ultimate, undiversified, eternal ground beyond which there appears to be nowhere to progress" (Lincoln Barnett); "an autonomous and regulating spiritual principle" (W. Heitler); "an invisible abyss of mystery . . . [an] immense, unknown realm of the mysterious" (A. Portmann).[58] A more universally used and all-embracing term for the numerous descriptions above is "the field": Akashic field (Ervin Laszlo), morphogenetic field (Rupert Sheldrake), unified field of pure consciousness (John Hagelin). The "field" (that I have come to identify with Rahner's Ground of Being) might best be described as the dynamic presence of everything that is, was, and ever will be. It holds the wisdom of the ages— all ages, everywhere and of time to come. It is, however, beyond time and space. It is envisioned by scientists as pure energy and light, interconnectedness, consciousness, love, relationality, infinity. In our way of thinking, it is the closest we can come metaphorically to speak of the Divine as the inescapable Holy pervading all, or perhaps, as the Mind of God holding within it all that is.

Jesus, I believe, knew who he was and lived what all of us are called to live, and can live, when we truly know who we are. Because of this, in his human form he radiated the Divine and manifested extraordinary energy and goodness.

Did the disciples recognize all of this in him? Not before his death, and only in a limited way after his resurrection, since we can see only within the context of our life, time, and space. Before his death they saw in him great goodness and were attracted to him and his energy, his teaching, and the lifestyle he modeled, as they understood it. After the resurrection experience, they saw him as the Messiah (in Greek, the Christ, the anointed one of God) as they understood that term then. Eventually, and for various reasons—some scholars, as I have already mentioned, speculate that it began as a nonviolent revolutionary "anti-'Caesar is Lord, son of god'" proclamation—they referred to him as Lord and Son of God, as the one they would follow. The meaning and depth of this, it must be stressed, evolved through the ages. We can already see major differences between the earlier Synoptic Gospels and John's Gospel at the end of the first century. The divinity of Jesus, however, was definitively formalized and explained in Greek metaphysical categories at the Council of Nicaea in the fourth century.

At this time in my life, I find that the formulations of Nicaea no longer touch me very deeply. Instead, I

find my deepest inspiration when I reflect on the resurrection experience (however one understands it) as
calling forth in the followers of Jesus an evolving and
ever deepening understanding of Jesus as the "Human
Being" whose life was vindicated by God. I say this without any desire to diminish the doctrinal statements of
the past stressing his divinity and oneness with God. My
personal emphasis on Jesus as the "Son of Humanity,"
the "human archetype"— manifesting for his followers, and also for us today, who we are also called to be,
arises out of my suspicion that our sometimes excessive
stress on his divinity has all too often alienated us from
Jesus. It seems too easy to use his divinity as an excuse
for why we cannot possibly be as forgiving, compassion-
ate, and faithful as he was. Jesus, I believe, modeled for
us the "human path." In that way, he called forth our
homecoming to ourselves, our salvation, and in the truest sense, therefore, also our divinization. His followers
wrote about this in the manner of their day, i.e., in parables and metaphor mainly. That is what the Gospels are:
they were intended not primarily as history, but rather as
revelation, as opening up who and how Jesus was—*for
our living* and for the *transformation of our humanity.*

THE COSMIC CHRIST

The Gospels, however, are never finished. Revelation
is ongoing and as we live and pray into the meaning of
Jesus as the Christ in our midst, we walk into his Story

and, by the power of his Spirit, make it our own. We tap into its energy field and expand its truth for us: Who Jesus was and calls us to be, thus, becomes *our* story— not primarily as historical, but in an archetypal, transhistorical way. This is happening all around us today, especially as human consciousness expands. It happens in the peace movement, in the martyrdom of Dorothy Stang and other justice workers throughout the world regardless of their denomination, in the soup kitchens in our inner cities, in healing practices that are becoming ever more holistic, in shelters for the homeless, for women in prostitution, for victims of human trafficking, in our prison ministries and in so many other works of mercy done in the name of love.

Tapping into the energy field of which we are in fact a part is tapping into the cosmic event that today some have come to call the "Christ Event" or the "Cosmic Christ." As Christians, we claim this as our reality here on this planet. Christ may not be a conscious reality for, or openly affect, other conscious life in the cosmos. In as much, however, as all is held in the "Field" that expands beyond our little globe into the universe and even beyond, Christ is present in the goodness that is manifest there as well. Christ is present also in the love and integrity of humans who are not Christians, whether they know of him or not. All teaching and learning that speaks to the fullness of our humanity is interconnected, and we can say therefore that it is of the Christ. It is, of course, of the Buddha as well, and of other authentic teachers. One does not rule out the other.

Regarding this last remark, it may be helpful to remind ourselves once again of the worldview of today that stresses the interconnectedness of everything in the universe. The paths of love are one, and human home-coming has but one destiny. In this regard, a transcript of an interesting interview by Leonardo Boff with the Dalai Lama was sent to me not long ago over the Internet. It was entitled: "Your_religion_not_important." In the interview Boff asks the Dalai Lama—a man well versed in the quantum perspective[59]—what, according to him, is the best religion. The Dalai Lama answers, quite sim-ply, that the best religion is the one that gets you closest to God, that makes you a better person. Boff then won-ders what it is that makes one a better person, and the Dalai Lama's response:

> Whatever makes you more compassionate, more sensible, more detached, more loving, more humanitarian, more responsible, more ethical. The religion that will do that for you is the best. I am not interested, my friend, about your reli-gion or if you are religious or not. . . . What really is important to me is your behavior. Remember the universe is the echo of our actions and our thoughts.

Following the path that Jesus modeled is for those of us who are Christians the path that the Dalai Lama described. Simply calling ourselves Christian and having a baptismal certificate to prove it does not make us so. Christianity is an action-oriented path, and our Christification lies in what we do. I see the Cosmic Christ, therefore, as the one whose Body we are ever more fully becoming (evolving into) in the manner discussed above, the one whose glory is in the realization of the love, the compassion, and the forgiveness modeled by the life and death of Jesus.

Christ then, for me, is the transtemporal archetype of divinized humanity. The story of Jesus, as we have come to understand it and are continuing to understand it in ever more profound ways, opens us up to this Cosmic Christ archetype and models the fullness of humanity for us. The "Omega Point," or end point, as Teilhard calls it,[60] happens when we as the human family have in fact "harnessed for God the energies of Love," when we have come home to what we truly are. This Omega Point, as I see it, is ultimate salvation.

9

ON BECOMING
WHO WE ARE:
DIVINITY UNFOLDING

The Guest is inside you, and also inside me;
you know the sprout is hidden inside the seed.

—Kabir, *Ecstatic Poems*

Not long ago while rummaging through one of my book-
cases to select books to give away, I came upon an old
German reader that years ago I had begged one of my sisters to part with and give to me, since I had dearly loved
one of its many stories and wanted to enjoy it once again.
The reader was a work of numerous essays, short stories, and selected poems by the great German masters:
Goethe, Schiller, Rilke, Hölderlin, and others. Return-
ing home and unpacking, I had put the book on one of
my bookshelves and, as so often happens in a busy life,
though I had looked at it from time to time, I had never
allowed myself the luxury of settling down and actually
reading my favorite story. This last time, however, as I
picked up the book once again, I could not resist.

The tale I read is one of extraordinary conversion, which gripped me at this last reading much more

profoundly than it had ever done in my youth. In fact, and to my amazement, it haunted me for days. What, above all, kept coming back to me and returned me to the story ever again, was a verse by Hölderlin uttered by the protagonist at the end of the story—a verse that as a young girl I could not possibly have grasped: *Those alone believe in the Divine who themselves are That.* (*An das Göttliche glauben die allein, die es selber sind.*)

QUESTIONS
IN A QUANTUM AGE

Some time after reading the story I went on retreat, leaving the German reader behind, but the Hölderlin verse would not let me go. It kept arising in my mind and stirring my heart, challenging me with its relevance during this time of solitude and silence. I had, of course, been questioning into the nature of the Divine consciously or semi-consciously for a long time and especially in the last few years when what I call the need for a *new way of seeing*—the urgency for a *transformation of consciousness* in this, the quantum age of the twentieth and twenty-first centuries—had increasingly pressed itself upon me. Clearly, there are numerous categories that need to be held within the embrace of a *transformation* such as this. Nevertheless, although a transformed search for the Sacred and for an encounter with the Holy is certainly the most important of these, it is not necessarily the first one we become aware of when we ponder the profound change that a totally new perspective on reality-as-a-whole necessitates. That, I believe, is why so many of us unfortunately stay at the circumference of life for a long time without ever realizing that we are missing the center.

In the past several years I had reflected often on, and also spoken about, how our lifestyle as citizens in this quantum age needs to change; how the insights into global interconnectedness affect our cherished individualism and mandate mutual responsibility; how identity issues are affected. I had probed into our cultural understanding of truth and our attachment to certainty, into our preference for permanence and resistance to change, into our notions of superiority and inferiority, objectivity and subjectivity, inclusion and exclusion. I had tried to address many of the social and religious standards that we have set up in the light of these understandings and have declared as inviolable. My ponderings about Christianity (specifically Catholicism) — about its official interpretations of creation and incarnation, of sin and redemption, of sacraments as means to the latter, of sacramental rites and the right to administer or receive them, of a Savior, Jesus of Nazareth in relation to the Christ, of death, eternity, and so much more—all clearly were affected by the need for change. Underlying everything, however, silently at first, but with an ever-greater intensity as I continued questioning, was my passionate search for a deeper understanding of the Divine itself.

As a Catholic, of course, laden with dogmatic conclusions from childhood, I initially wondered:

1. How one might humbly approach this Mystery, dwell there in peace-filled *tentativeness* and endure its luring, always *remaining on the quest*—with a burning hope for yet "a better dawn";

2. How one could honestly and openly do this within the framework of a religion

   ♦ that speaks of certainties and dogmatizes them;

   ♦ that declares itself as "the (new) chosen people," intentionally established by the Son of God, and knows exactly what that means;

   ♦ that dialogues always, with a desire to convert rather than with a longing for deeper insights— as a pilgrim people journeying *into* the Mystery with others, rather than possessing it;

3. How one could speak or write of the searing yet ecstatic pain of questing, without forever making sure that one reassured everyone that what one was writing was "rooted in tradition"—had, in other words, already been mentioned by some holy man, declared a "Father or Doctor of the church" long ago—a man who belonged, as we all know ever more clearly now, to another age and culture and, therefore, in many respects, could not possibly, and without any wrongdoing on his part, have seen what was revealing itself in our time.

I finally concluded that: When something is truly new, it is precisely that. Why then, I asked myself, should "revelation" always find its authorization in the old, in the past, in bygone days? Why should the old, the ancient, necessarily be holier than the new? Does not the Christ belong to yesterday, today, and into the future—the Alpha and the Omega, and *everything that reveals itself in between?*

What then do the words of Hölderlin ("Those alone believe in the Divine who themselves are That.") mean for us as children in an expanding, unfolding universe; as part of that universe —"stardust" become conscious of the glory and the ecstasy of this unfolding? Without repeating here, but simply recalling for ourselves, the findings of an ever developing cosmology and of the quantum perspective emerging in our time that I and others have dealt with elsewhere,[61] could we not suggest that Hölderlin's words invite us to see Divinity permeating each one of us in every aspect of our being, and that our capacity for true belief is predicated on the reality of that permeation as an *essential* dimension of who we are?

◆ "I in God and God in me."

◆ "Deep calls unto deep."

Or, might one, perhaps a bit less reverently, suggest:

◆ "It takes one to know One"?

Authentic faith is born there. Hölderlin received this insight "as a lightning flash," in all humility, or, as he would say, "bare-headed and with arms outstretched," and passed it on "in song to the world" (as indeed only great poets can).

THE FEAR OF PANTHEISM

"Are you courting pantheism?" some might ask me at this point. My answer, right now, is that I really am not sure anymore, as I live into what scientific research is offering us today. We live in a time of "bridging," knowing what we know today and at the same time being consciously aware of a time in our life when we had very different perspectives. As a child around eleven or so, while still in Germany, I used to visit an elegant, well-educated, young woman some fifteen or more years my senior. She was a friend of my parents, who, I had overheard, was suffering from a painful and broken love relationship. I somehow, innocently, felt that my presence would comfort her in her pain. Although she never mentioned her broken relationship to me, a mere child, we did talk of various rather profound matters that should really have been way beyond me. Pantheism was one topic. She believed in it. I, a good Catholic girl, did not, and I remember secretly praying for her conversion. When I think of her today, many years and experiences later and immersed, as I am, in a very different world perspective, I honestly doubt that she needed my prayers.

Naïve pantheism that equates everything with *the* God, often solidifying any object as worthy of adoration ("all equals God") if this is what some actually understand by pantheism, is clearly not what I am thinking about. But after the discovery of the hologram, with theories concerning the holographic nature of the universe, the brain, and possibly all of reality; with the realization that the whole, indeed, *is in each of its parts*,[62] what can possibly be the problem with seeing Divinity "parenting" all of creation (pan*en*theism?) and, therefore, giving us *itself* in *every part* of our being? *"Those alone believe in the Divine who themselves are That."*

The equally true scientific insight of today, claiming paradoxically that the whole is *greater that the sum of its parts*, should in turn stretch us even further and deepen our appreciation for the transcendent power behind evolution—divine love energy, ever drawing us beyond ourselves into itself as our own destiny already present within the totality of who we are. It should, furthermore, allay any fear of exaggerated self-aggrandizement that might mistakenly result from a holographic spiritual perspective. Instead, it might evoke ever more deeply the hunger and longing that lies at the base of our vocation to *become who we truly are,* having us exult in being part of the divine unfolding.

METAPHOR AS GOD LANGUAGE

All God language, is of course, always and of necessity metaphor. It points to the *Yes* and also always holds it in tension with the *No* of whatever it is describing. It finds its home in Heidegger's *Alétheia*—the "unconcealing-concealment": A dynamic of revelation and withholding, of darkness and light in constant interplay with Mystery, where, in the recognition of our poverty and of the dearth of our understanding, we gain wisdom, where, in acknowledged hunger and thirst, we experience the banquet. The poet Rilke, in his praise of darkness, helps us ponder this:

> You darkness whence I came,
> I love you more than the flame
> that surrounds the world,
> since she can illumine
> any one circle with her light
> outside of which no one can know her.

> But the darkness draws all to herself:
> shapes and flames, animals and me,
> how quickly she gathers
> mortals and might—

> And I can sense a powerful presence
> surrounding me.

> I believe in the night.

> > —Rainer Maria Rilke, *"Du Dunkelheit"*
> > from *Stundenbuch*, trans. mine

Sadly, however, in this process of ongoing revelation—of the light and darkness interplay, we often mistakenly focus exclusively on a visual or conceptual detail and therefore do not truly *experience* the whole. We fixate and hold on to the light, deny darkness, and claim we "have" the whole truth. In our haste to grasp and hold on, we miss the point: the underlying wisdom, the depth perspective, the bigger picture. We worry then about vocabulary, the correct way of speaking about the God of revelation, the proper rituals and gestures to be used in worship—as if God (who, as the poet Rumi assures us, "looks only for the burning heart," for its yearning and its questing and hears not the words we say) actually cared. We fixate on the moment, on what has come to us, on what must be dealt with expeditiously right then and needs to be concretized and categorized to suit our comfort level. In this way we succeed, of course, in avoiding the pain of darkness and waiting, but we also miss the beauty—the much more significant and ever flowing, the constantly transforming event of revelation.

A father and a king, a throne on which he sits, positions of honor at his right or left hand, a judgment day, places of reward and punishment, and so many more creedal assertions are merely metaphoric ways of expressing our feeble human attempts at understanding and approaching what ultimately is beyond words and the categories of our mind. They are human constructs, no more than that, and should be treated that way—as time-bound anthropomorphisms, projections of our momentary experience of reality. They are images suited to an ancient context, to one particular period in history no longer available to us except in fairy-tales or national monarchies nostalgically held on to for "patriotism" and pride of heritage, but otherwise possessing only the power of fantasy. They are quaint at best but foreign, really, to us in our time. To absolutize them and mindlessly proclaim them as the content and rubrics of our religion, professions of our faith, eternal verities that cannot change, is in today's world incomprehensible.

I listen to the Nicene Creed we are invited to recite every Sunday—recently made even more convoluted through Latin adaptations. Sometimes I try to change the wording in order to be able to say it still, in a manner more meaningful at least to me. I wonder whether many there, present with me in the pews, feel like I do; whether many just move into a state of mindlessness that can endure the words; whether others simply no longer care. I know that a number of theologians and spiritual writers of our time have attempted to work with the broader meaning of the creed in order to make it more relevant. I myself have in the past given retreats on the "tenets" of our faith and, without going through the text of the creed word for word, have addressed the broader categories present there. Today I no longer sense that there is great interest in this, most definitely not among the young, but also among adults who are puzzled at best but have grown disenchanted with an ecclesial leadership that seems simply to plod along, expecting us to do the same, and holding fast to what was—sacred images of bygone days that no longer nourish anyone.

Gratefully, there are today a large number of excellent exegetical works, especially since the Second Vatican Council, that explain the literary genre, the culture and meaning, of the Christian scriptures. They address their intent, their linguistic characteristics, their interdependence or lack thereof, their historical contexts. Those serious about their faith, therefore, readily have access to readable material where they can discover that—when they read about how Jesus spoke of God, of the Kingdom, of the forgiving Father, and when he told parables—Jesus expressed symbolically what he saw and how he understood the tender mercy and compassion of the creative and all embracing Divine-Unfolding that could not otherwise be encapsulated in finitude. His were not concrete, factual realities but metaphoric, parabolic pointers to the profound Mystery of Love that calls us to move ever more deeply into the reality of the Divine.

ON TOUCHING THE HEART

Because of the Hellenic overlay on much of the original Christian writings, it is difficult for us to grasp at first that Jesus of Nazareth was not primarily a teacher of concepts. He was a teacher and prophet of action and

societal transformation. Conceptual categories can and
do change with time and when overemphasized can
wither the heart. I believe that language and symbols,
especially as Jesus used them, were meant primarily to
deepen our relation with one another, to "com-*uni*-cate,"
to unite us and grow us. Jesus meant to touch and trans-
form our heart (one of the primary organs of contact
with reality).

Our heart, much more importantly than our intellect, our mind, was of concern to Jesus. We say, quite
rightly, that actions speak louder than words. Jesus was
a man of vision, concerned primarily for the "reign of
God," not as a concept, but as a living, ever transforming
reality that would bring justice to an oppressive world
order, change the way we related with each other, and
gentle all of us. He spoke his vision with conviction,
and he lived it—healing the sick, the downtrodden, and
ostracized of his day. With integrity (not violence), Jesus
challenged the domination system of his time.

When language about God becomes purely conceptual, it can easily lend itself to argument and dogmatic absolutes that assault the Sacred and immobilize
the heart, hinder the freedom of questing, and destroy
authentic faith. Then we ultimately have no choice
except to turn away and steep ourselves in silence. That
is at least one reason why some actually prefer the latter
whenever they are moved to pray. Authentic faith origi-
nates and ends in inner stillness where alone the abyss

of Mystery can unfold. It is my sense that when forced to speak (something that our communal and linguistic nature ultimately demands of us), authentic faith-expression should always be tentative, and its symbols momentary. It should, as Heidegger would say, ever be "faith in the face of doubt," of uncertainty; faith faced with the "cloud of unknowing"; faith that has encountered Mystery and dwells there.

Hölderlin's saying then, *Those alone believe in the Divine who themselves are That,* points clearly beyond the mundane, the convenient, the worldly, the wordy and purely literal. He is not referring to a pantheon of gods that "have got it," as different from those of us who have not. He is referring to the inner fire that burns and sears, that destroys "things" and makes room for the *"No-thing"* where the Sacred finds its abode. It is a fire that will not let us go, because it is within all of us and, once awakened, will not rest until we take the "leap into the Absurd" that Kierkegaard talks about, where finally intellect yields to Love, and God becomes human, emerging in, and divinizing, all of us.

10

APPROACHING THE MYSTERY

Holy Mystery beyond our knowing, . . .
You are Life, Energy, Beauty, Wisdom,
Impenetrable Mystery.
In humility we praise the wonder
of your creation,
and seek only to play our natural
and love-designed role here
in reverence and gratitude.
Amen.

—William Cleary,
Prayers to an Evolutionary God

I have thought long and hard, not only about a possible title for this brief essay but, more importantly, about even daring to write anything at all. In all my retreats and workshops when I speak of "new ways of seeing" and approaching the Divine, I point to symbols and metaphors as the only way humans can talk about God. I speak of the poverty of human language, of its abuse in our constant quest for certainty, and of our persistent temptation to retreat into absolutes and to persuade others that we have the answer: simple or complicated, that we have what it takes to identify who God is: male, father almighty, judge, mighty fortress, *homoousios*, three in one, "consubstantial" with each other, and so on. I maintain that God is ineffable—not a problem to be solved, not some divine entity to be defined. God, I say, is an alluring mystery ever to be entered in upon. I suggest that when we speak of God, the best approach would most likely be through the heart, through a sense of the Holy that pervades our experience, not through categories of reason—often dry and not "prayer-inspiring." I insist also that the ecstasy is in the journey and that the way of silence and gentle waiting may ultimately be the most profound form of praise, thanksgiving, and communion.

Yet here I am, trying to respond to the question that persists: can we not gain at least some glimpse, are there not at least some metaphors that might be helpful for our time—that move beyond the Greco-Roman or mediaeval categories of kingship and thrones, places of privilege, right and left hand, up and down, and so forth? Are we not symbol makers, I ask myself, social beings who need to express themselves about the important realities in their lives? God, above all, is an issue, an allure for me and, I hope also, for those who will read these musings. How do we move, then, beyond the absolutized deity of religion (a God in man's trousers sitting in heavenly glory) and humbly approach the "Ground of

Being" that Rahner mentions, but that leaves so many of us puzzled because we want a "personal" God— someone with whom we can speak like we speak to our parents or friends? There is a certain frustration in this question since even the word "personal" is already an anthropomorphism, and so I wonder whether there is another way to satisfy the human longing for closeness and intimacy with the Divine, without picturing an individual or individuals as humans have done since time immemorial.

As Christians we have, of course, Jesus, who, we believe, is the fullest manifestation of the Divine here on earth. We also have Mary, the mother of Jesus, who with Joseph encouraged his maturation into God. We have the saints, our departed loved ones—saints also, and the angels. However, *God*—how can we approach the Holy One and not "thingify" or, as the philosophers say, "reify" the Divine? How can we refrain from turning God into someone like us, just more "unlike than like" or "infinitely more so"? Theologians call this approach "analogy" and have struggled with similarity and dissimilarity ever since the earliest days of theology.[63]

This is not the first time I have struggled with this question, either. After all, every religious category from creation, through sin and punishment, to redemption uses human concepts—a God image that is projected outward onto God in a manner deemed appropriate for whatever culture conceives of it:

◆ If we want someone punished for crimes committed against us, we will argue God would wish this also: "May you burn in hell!" is a perfect example of how we accommodate God's justice to our human need for vengeance.

◆ "Why would God send him so much suffering? He is such a good man," we say. The statement stems directly from our view of *punishment and justice* that we attribute to God—in this case finding fault with God for punishing unjustly. This statement, of course, also refers indirectly to our interpretation of salvation discussed earlier (chapter 6).

◆ We turn God into a Father (Agrarian Age) or a Mother (pre-Agrarian times) depending on the cultural understanding of power and our own personal dependence on its benevolence.

◆ We see God as walking among us, dwelling on Mount Olympus, or being above us in the heavens—depending on our cosmology.

The examples can go on and on. They are not to be spurned, as some atheists would insist. Humans are linguistic beings with imagination and intellect, whose communal nature drives them to share insights and look for meaning. When the empirical fails us, we move quite naturally beyond it to the symbolic, metaphorical, or analogical. We also may simply remain silent in the face of a Mystery that cannot be explained, yet continues to fascinates us, precisely because it is not beyond experience but simply beyond explanation. So here we are, once again, back where we started: the apophatic approach of silence and waiting, or the frustrating use of personal symbols that we know, deep down, no longer satisfy us, largely because of their inadequacy and their oppressive and exclusive use that has alienated us from them in search of some better way of approaching the Mystery.

I do believe that moving from the "Father/Mother" image, or the "Lord, Son, Word of God" theology, to the divine Spirit may be of some help here. In the early morning hours not long ago when this very Spirit always seems freer to penetrate my still sleepy mind just slowly waking up, a poem by Gerald Manley Hopkins came to me:

The world is charged with the grandeur of God.
It will flame out, like shining from shook foil;
It gathers to a greatness, like the ooze of oil
Crushed. Why do men then now not reck his rod?
Generations have trod, have trod, have trod;
And all is seared with trade; bleared, smeared with toil;
And wears man's smudge and shares man's smell: the soil
Is bare now, nor can foot feel, being shod.

And for all this, nature is never spent;
There lives the dearest freshness deep down things;
And though the last lights off the black West went
Oh, morning, at the brown brink eastward, springs—
Because the Holy Ghost over the bent
World broods with warm breast and with ah! bright wings.

(italics mine)

Hopkins was a "see-er." This is his most famous poem, I suppose, but many of his others invite us to look and to see as well. And what is it that he wants us to see but the power of the Divine, the Holy One, the Spirit—what others have called the Presence, the silent Ground, that holds all in its being.

As I am writing this I am sitting at my window. Outside it is a foggy, dark, rainy day. Across the alley are bushes, tall, bare trees, and a soggy hillside of winter grass. At other times I would have seen it all as quite depressing— one more day of rain and clouds. But today something makes me pull up the shades and has me spend some time looking—gazing is perhaps a better word. All I can say is: "You, my God, are beautiful even in this apparent sadness." I am reminded of a poster I had received many years ago. It was a picture of an old rusty truck—just one wheel and part of the cab and motor showing. They were mired in dirt. A little white flower was peeping out of the dirt close to the rusty wheel, and the words of Gerald Manley Hopkins were printed at the bottom of the picture: "The world is charged with the grandeur of God."

THE GODS HAVE FLED

In our reflections concerning religious idols (chapter 3), I referred to Martin Heidegger's observation that the gods seem to have fled at this time in human history. He suggested in *Holzwege* (published in 1950) what may even be more deeply distressing, namely, that not only is God

absent in modern times, but that in fact the radiance of
divinity itself has been extinguished in world history.[64]
Today, some sixty years after he wrote this, more and
more of us might agree with him as we experience alienation and a deep hunger for the truly holy in many of
our religions where the "gods" indeed seem to have fled
both from our churches and even our hearts. A strange
event, however, is happening today, and Heidegger fore-
saw this as well; for even as we find ourselves in destitute times—hungering for depth, though perhaps barely
aware of this in the performance of our canonical obligations—there slowly seems to be opening up for us, out of
this very destitution and hunger, room for an encounter with the Divine. It would seem that barrenness and
darkness and the consequent sorrow and suffering are
necessary at times to allow for the breakthrough of new
life and light. God seems infinitely patient in this regard.
Perhaps the decline of cultures or institutions and cherished institutionalized ways of praise and worship, even
if it upsets many of us, is really not offensive to God who,
as scripture suggests, is indifferent to sacrifice and obla-
tions and looks instead for the burning heart.

There is in the foundational thought of Heidegger
a simple way of reflecting on this: He suggests that
our usual way of thinking and encountering the world
around us is by way of objectification and "commodifi-
cation." We see our reality and classify it in terms of the
favorable and unfavorable, the quantifiable, measurable,

explainable, definable, controllable, and ordered. We understand *beings* in terms of their separate-ness. We distinguish and define and, in doing so, we labor under the illusion that we can grasp what we see and comprehend it. We do this with things, with animals, and also with persons, their communities, their countries, their cultures. We even do this with the "object" of our theological investigations, God, and our relation to "Him." The more we have (possessions, knowledge), the more we want control—a need that becomes insatiable, a destitution that can never be healed. Kierkegaard describes the end result of such an approach as a "sickness unto death." Frankl sees it as "existential boredom "—the "unheard [or unrecognized] cry for meaning." In that way, according to Hopkins, "generations have trod, have trod, have trod."

The question that could lead to healing and could help us "find rest" does not seem to occur too readily to many of us. It is a depth question centered in wonder and asks quite simply—but also surprisingly for those who "take things for granted:

- How it is that there is *anything at all?*

- How it is that beings *are?*

- What allows them *to be?*

An easy and quick answer that has been given often and for a long time now is that a Supreme Being—a God— does. But would that not make God just one more thing, a being among other beings, just greater? The question then persists and must be asked again:

♦ How is it that this *supreme* being is?

All sorts of explanations have been offered through the ages to answer this question as well, but no matter what has been tried, God somehow always was reduced to "someone like us"—a definite person, a father/mother, a judge, a king, an uncaused cause, an unmoved mover, etc. We say God is transcendent, but we are not satisfied unless the transcendent looks and feels somehow like us anyway.

Heidegger and others have argued that by so doing the Mystery escapes us, or perhaps better said: *the Mystery withdraws, flees,* or *conceals itself.* Because we can no longer see it, we delude ourselves into thinking that *the Mystery* no longer exists, that it has been solved, and we begin to live in a type of "forgetfulness," blindness, that parades as sight. He suggests that in our eagerness to control and get a hold of things, we have not as yet *thought* the *dynamic,* the process of Being itself. We seem, therefore, thoughtlessly lost in the midst of *beings* (things)—how to define them, understand them, use them, quantify, order, and control them.

An example regarding our God-relationship, which has in our time progressively been objectified and "rubricized," may be helpful here: As I reflect on the "new" language in our liturgy, it is interesting how our ecclesial "reforms" increasingly manifest a total unawareness of the difference between the words used in the "official" prayers mandated, and the ineffable Mystery they are meant to mediate. By unwittingly equating one with the other, the "reformers" have fallen victim to a pietistic absolutism: verbiage that ultimately alienates us from, rather than brings us closer to, the Holy—waiting to embrace us. In depth prayer this difference is revealed and at the same time *bridged*. In pietism, language replaces the unspeakable Mystery rather than humbly pointing toward it. By accentuating what is deemed "proper," one separates it from the Divine it is meant to reveal. Thus, one achieves the exact opposite of what is intended. Our words then merely blur our vision and we feel alienated, abandoned, and alone. We experience the blear, smear, smudge, and smell that Hopkins speaks about and lose sight of the grandeur, the greatness, and ultimately the "dearest freshness deep down things."

On the day that we dare take the leap away from a reified God, the "object" of theological speculation; on the day that we dare allow ourselves to approach, in other words, and deeply to meditate Being—as the sacred presencing of all that is—*not as a thing*, but, perhaps more accurately put, *as an event, as an ongoing process of appearing, of emerging*, we might, actually, find ourselves in the extraordinary dynamic of creation itself with all its power, its energy, its glory, and its mystery. For this, however, it is imperative that we understand Being as a *letting be of everything that is*, a happening and empowering of all. (The word "Be-ing" is a gerund and here should be seen as a verbal noun—a movement, an event, a happening.) Being is presencing the way I tried to discuss it in *Embraced by Compassion* many years ago: It is Presence as an event that transcends the boundaries of space and time, the here and the now that "calls us forth from within, even as it encounters us [and all that is] from without. We touch it at our center and from there are moved beyond ourselves. Unsolicited as well as unexpected, it embraces and holds us, and yet it sets us [and everything that is] free."[65] It grounds us, and all of "creation," and releases us simultaneously. It reveals and withholds itself beyond our control.

Ralph Harper sees this event as "a unitary experience and an experience of totality in the midst of shattering differences."[66] And this brings us back to Hopkins's "There lives the dearest freshness deep down things." He calls the ground and source of this freshness the Holy Ghost. He is right, of course, as long as we do not objectify the Divine once again taking a poetic symbol and reducing it by imagining the Spirit (Ghost) as a dove.

I believe that as mysterious, paradoxical, and even somewhat complicated as our above reflections may have been, it is nevertheless important for our time of destitution and hunger that we allow ourselves, in spite of the pain or desolation we may initially feel, to dwell in the Mystery that this revelation of Being opens up

- as No-*Thing* that, nevertheless, allows all things to be;

- as a "letting be" of what is, a flow, an emerging;

- as an empowering and releasing of the entire universe into freedom.

- as a love act from the tender power of our creator God.

We may then be able in gentle stillness and deep reverence to experience the holiness of this ongoing event. And there we may at last be ready for a revelation of the Divine—an un-concealing and opening up for us of the Holy Mystery. John V. Taylor said it well many years ago: "The adult mind must be unstriving, receptive, expectant, before there can be creative insight. . . . We do not work it out; rather we have a sense of waiting for the disclosure of something that is already there.[67]

Words will clearly fail us here, because words speak of "things." Silence and awe will be our best response—an immersion, a surrender, a drowning in, a prostration in utter self-gift and ultimately, a dwelling there. That is perhaps the best way of describing what prayer will then be like:

> *No gift is proper to a Deity;*
> *no fruit is worthy for such power to bless.*
> *If you have nothing, gather back your sigh,*
> *and with your hands held high, your heart held high,*
> *lift up your emptiness!*
>
> —Jessica Powers[68]

We are vessels. Our being is receptivity wherein "re-collection" can happen. Our emptiness as ready openness to the Divine is our prayer, our thanksgiving.

VIRGIN MOTHERING

There is perhaps no one who has come closer to describing the disposition necessary to allow for a depth experience and encounter with the Holy One than the thirteenth-century Dominican mystic Meister Eckhart. He was a preacher, one of the first to preach in the vernacular so that those attending Eucharist could actually understand what he was saying rather than be reduced to passivity in having to sit through a homily delivered in Latin and accessible only to the learned.

In one of his German sermons, Eckhart compares human receptivity and openness to the Divine to the empty clarity of a mirror. What do we see when we look into a mirror, he wonders. It is clear that we do not primarily see the mirror, which is noticed only when it distorts our countenance in some way by being smudged, scratched, chipped, or dirty. If the mirror is what a mirror is meant to be, it is, empty and clear, pure receptivity that renders back to us who gaze into it our countenance, So, he claims, it must be with our soul. Like Mary, the Mother of Jesus, we are meant to be virgin souls, Eckhart insists. When God looks at us we are called to give back to God, God's very countenance. God gazes at us, and all of creation (*recognized by us, held in our consciousness as resplendent in infinite diversity and holiness)* is reflected back to God. In this way through our empty openness and grateful receptivity we birth God back to God. We become as Mary was, virgin mothers. Our call as human openness to the Divine is meant to be the silent place of God's presence. By our "Yes" (*fiat*) to the Divine break-through nothing other than God remains in us. We receive our being from God, and our being, in empty openness, is God's presence. Thus we are children of God—those who from God are what they are and noth-ing else. As virgin souls, however, we also "mother" God. We are pure presence of the Mystery.

Eckhart expands the "virgin mother" metaphor in still another sermon that is perhaps a bit clearer because it is more concrete. He meditates on the Gospel of Luke 10:38: "Now as they went on their way, he entered a cer-tain village, where a woman named Martha welcomed him into her home." He wonders what kind of a home it would have to be for Jesus to feel welcome and then quickly moves beyond the physical dwelling into the home of our hearts, our souls. He pictures a welcoming soul, once again as one that is empty and then quickly gets to the point by describing this emptiness as freedom from all assumptions, presuppositions, expectations, and prejudices of what anything or anyone should be. He reminds us that in God's creation, God breaks out in infi-nite diversity and can never be limited by our rules and regulations regarding propriety, goodness, and beauty.

God's breakthrough does not know superiority and inferiority, rightness and wrongness. Our assumptions and
prejudices, therefore, serve only to limit the revelation
of God's multifaceted self-bestowal in creation. They
impoverish us and belie the divine presence.

As welcoming souls we are to be as empty as a virgin
awaiting the seed, released from everything that might
restrict divine abundance, released from all that can prevent us from accepting the Holy as it reveals itself in all
of creation. We stand with arms outstretched, receiving
the sacred breakthrough in praise and in thanksgiving.
As such, says Eckhart, we are not only virgins but we
become "virgin mothers." We let *how* God is in creation
be. We empower and enhance what is as it is. "Let a river
be a river; let a mountain be a mountain," he says, do not
turn nature into a polluted, wounded, broken world. I
would add: let your neighbor be your neighbor, let your
child be your child, let your spouse be your spouse. Do
not turn the world into your image and likeness. See it
and honor it as the breakthrough of God. Let cultures
and nationalities and diverse religions be what they are.
Let them praise God in their way. Let God be God in
them, through them, and for them.

In one of his reflections Eckhart says boldly, "I pray
God to rid me of God." As shocking as this may sound,
what he aims for is the inner freedom not to fixate on
one version of God—of what or who God should be, on
one place alone where God reveals God's self. He does

not want to impose any one version on others or even on himself that would then impede his openness to revelation as it continues to unfold. We welcome God into our souls, as did the Virgin Mary, when we celebrate God's infinite diversity in creation, when we allow for differences, rejoicing in creation as it is: God's outpouring in our children, our spouses, our co-workers, our sisters and brothers. We are true virgin souls when we let the world give itself to us as it is, not as we expect it to be, rejecting it if it is not what we think it should be. We are not meant to turn anyone into our image and likeness. We are to let God be God on this earth by shepherding creation in love, reverence, generosity, and respect, by learning from it how it should be encountered.[69]

The optometrist Jacob Liberman mentions in his book *Light, Medicine of the Future* that we need to *see* rather than to *look* at things. He invites us to gaze, if you will, and receive the world as it gives itself to us, rather than project our expectations of the world onto it while we miss what is really there.

> It is imperative that we "evolve" ourselves, integrating everything that allows us to become whole, more relational, and aware of our global community. Our task is to take in and to utilize light so that we may merge with our true selves and our destiny, thus facilitating the healing of the planet. As each of us becomes whole, we radi-

ate light—light from within—unimpeded by our self-imposed emotional and physical blocks.[70]

As Eckhart's virgin souls, we radiate that light, see God breaking out everywhere, and honor God *there* because we are empty of our own agenda. Listening to the other as other and receiving, as well as affirming this otherness, the virgin then becomes mother. Filled with the Divine, we become God-bearers, God affirmers in this world.

THE SIN OF THE WORLD

The sins that deny virgin motherhood can perhaps best be described as the "will to power" and ingratitude—the forgetfulness of our place in the Heart of God. A consequent insecurity has us want to be like God. We "stuff ourselves with stuff"—the "sickness unto death" we discussed earlier—and we try to turn the world and everyone in it into our image and likeness. Redemption can come to us only as we remember our place in creation, celebrate our emptiness, and gratefully acknowledge the divine Giver.

One of the most intriguing examples of the alienation that befalls us when ambition, the need to be right, to be in control, to win at any cost takes over in our togetherness with others is given by Jacques Lusseyran whom, together with Liberman, I have mentioned in a number of my other books. Blinded at the age of eight, Lusseyran made the amazing discovery very early into his total blindness that he was being guided by an inner light that peopled his inner world and serenely guided him through his outer one. Because of it, he was capable of navigating the world around him quite freely, to play and do ordinary things children do. The only condition necessary for this freedom was open receptivity and reverence for everything and everyone he encountered. When he grew afraid or doubted his inner guide, when he hesitated and imagined the world a hostile place, it seemed to become precisely that. He hit, scratched, or injured himself. Interestingly, anger, impatience, ambition, jealousy, or an unfriendly attitude had the same effect. Serenity, harmony, and good will toward his neighbor and all his surroundings had to be primary in his life for him to function effectively. They became indispensable in his relationships.[71] They are indispensable to all of us as well.

THE PRIMACY OF LOVE

The integrity of creation, as Teilhard de Chardin tells us, heralds the primacy of love. In *From Religion Back to Faith*, I discussed in some detail Beatrice Bruteau's explanation of how Teilhard sees love as the driving principle of evolution, which takes place through the "creative unions" of simple elements toward the more complex in constant movement toward ever higher consciousness. Love is the foundational power fueling this union through the attraction of characteristic energies and because of natural affinities. One might say that evolution would not happen without love—"the self-gift toward ever greater union and for the sake of greater consciousness" implanted in creation by its Source. "For Teilhard, creation is progression, with ever greater interiority and self-possession, toward community."[72]

Community in its most authentic sense is the manifestation of love in an ever-evolving cosmos. Lusseyran in his vulnerable state became intensely aware of the essential place this love has in all of life. The light within him was the manifestation, or root, of everything that is, as love. When he failed to recognize this he could not function. Because most of us are less sensitive than the blind child of eight, we do not always realize the distortion we create in the universe through our impatience, selfishness, ambition, anger, and lack of kindness, through our betrayal of love. We blindly proceed on our way into alienation, sighted though we are. Our homecoming, however, lies in reappropriating the call to virgin-mothering. It refers us to our grounding in the depth relationship we have with a Love ever present and waiting. We live and move and have our being there.

THOUGHTS AND QUESTIONS
FOR MEDITATION

1. "Encounter," the "I-Thou experience". . . all of us
    must admit that anything truly significant and life-
    changing in human existence always begins that
    way." Do you agree?

2. "Jesus, I believe, knew who he was and lived what
    all of us are called to live, and can live, when we
    truly know who we are." What does that mean?
    "Because of this, he radiated divine presence and
    manifested extraordinary energy and goodness."
    Can this happen for us?

3. How do you relate to the discussion of the develop-
    ment of Christology through the ages, rather than
    as an acknowledged reality for the disciples before
    the death and resurrection of Jesus?

4. How do you understand Jesus as "the Son of
    Humanity, the human archetype"?

5. Can you relate to the notion of the "Cosmic Christ"?
    Comment.

6. What is your response to the view of the Dalai Lama
    about religion?

7. "Those alone believe in the Divine who are them-
    selves That." What do you think Hölderlin meant by
    that? Does the discussion on the hologram help in

your understanding of your relation to the Divine? How can we be part of the divine unfolding?

8. Does the description of revelation as the "light and darkness interplay" make sense to you? Is the notion of metaphor in our God language helpful?

9. How can Hopkins help us see the divine presence in our midst beyond our usual need to anthropomorphize?

10. I reflected on Heidegger speaking of "the no-more of the gods that have fled and the *not-yet* of the god to come," by suggesting that "in many of our religions where the "gods" indeed seem to have fled both from our churches and even our hearts, a strange event, however, is happening today, . . . for even as we find ourselves in destitute times—hungering for depth, though perhaps barely aware of this in the performance of our canonical obligations—there slowly seems to be opening up for us, out of this very destitution and hunger, room for an encounter with the Divine." Do you see this in your life? If so, how?

11. How do you see the connection between the meditation on "Presence," on "Be-ing," on Gerald Manley Hopkins's *There lives the dearest freshness deep down things,* as well as on John V. Taylor's observation that "the adult mind must be unstriving, receptive, expectant, before there can be creative

insight. . . . We do not work it out; rather we have a sense of waiting for the disclosure of something that is already there"?

12. Was the mirror analogy for our openness to God's self-revelation helpful to you?

13. Meister Eckhart's Virgin Mother metaphor, clearly in praise of Mary the Mother of Jesus, combines emptiness with fruitfulness and proclaims it as necessary for all of us in our response to the Divine breakthrough in our lives. How has this reflection affected you?

14. What does Eckhart mean by his observation: "I pray God to rid me of God"?

15. "The will to power is the sin of the world." Is this true in your experience?

16. "Our homecoming, however, lies in reappropriating the call to virgin-mothering. It refers us to our grounding in the depth relationship we have with a Love ever present and waiting. We live and move and have our being there." What does this statement mean to you?

NOTES

Notes to Chapter 1

1. See Theresia M. Quigley, *I Cry for Innocence* (Saint John, New Brunswick: Dreamcatcher, 2002).

2. Ervin Laszlo, *Science and the Akashic Field: An Integral Theory of Everything* (Rochester, Vt.: Inner Traditions, 2004), 151–53.

3. Barbara Fiand, *From Religion Back to Faith: A Journey of the Heart* (New York: Crossroad, 2006), 140.

Notes to Chapter 2

4. Mircea Eliade, *Patterns in Comparative Religion* (Cleveland: Meridian Books, 1966). The entire book is a study of the sacred in the cosmos and of the sacred symbols humankind has used through the ages to honor this and to center ourselves there.

5. Peter Mayer, "Everything Is Holy Now," on the CD *Million Year Mind* (Stillwater, Minn.: P.O. Box 848), co-producer: Mark Anderson. A YouTube video presentation of this song is available on the Internet. Printed with permission.

Notes to Chapter 3

6. Martin Heidegger, *Vorträge und Aufsätze*, 3 vols., 3rd ed. (Pfullingen: Verlag Günther Neske, 1967), 1:100 (translation mine).

7. This term is used as a synonym for "infallibility" and should not be confused with its theological use referring to biblical freedom from error. See Christopher Begg, *The New Dictionary of Theology*, ed. Joseph A. Komonchak, Mary Collins, Dermot Lane (Wilmington, Del.: Michael Glazier, 1987), 515.

8. Martin Heidegger, *Existence and Being*, trans. Douglas Scott (Chicago: Henry Regney, Gateway, 1965), 289 (italics added).

9. *The Essential Rumi*, trans. Coleman Barks with John Moyne (New York: Harper Collins, 1995), 165–68.

10. John Shelby Spong, *Why Christianity Must Change or Die* (New York: HarperCollins, 1998), 47.

11. I am indebted for my explanation of metaphor to Sandra Schneiders, *The Revelatory Text* (San Francisco: HarperCollins, 1991), 29–33.

12. Garry Wills, *Papal Sin, Structures of Deceit* (New York: Doubleday, 2000), 214. See also August Bernhard Hasler, *How the Pope Became Infallible: Pius IX and the Politics of Persuasion* (Garden City, N.Y.: Doubleday, 1981), 178. In *The Papal No*, Deborah Halter claims that Pius IX did consult the world's bishops (New York: Crossroad, 2004), 118. In an article published in *L'Osservatore Romano*, the Italian historian Francesco Gugglietta claims consultation as well (Catholic News Agency, February 13, 2008). This consultation was in the form of a letter sent to the bishops asking them if the faithful in their dioceses favored the dogma. A majority of those asked replied in the affirmative, but theological discussion was rejected both with the opposition as well as with the theologians (especially in Germany), who objected to the dogma largely on historical grounds.

13. For an extensive discussion on the changing theories about early abortion in the Christian tradition and the long-held theory of "ensoulment" see Maggie Hume: "The Shifting Ground of Contraception" in *Rome Has Spoken: A Guide to Forgotten Papal Statements, and How They Have Changed through the Centuries,* ed. Maureen Fiedler and Linda Rabben (New York: Crossroad, 1998), 152–58. For an additional well-documented account of this issue see also Joanna Manning, *Take Back the Truth: Confronting Papal Power and the Religious Right* (New York: Crossroad, 2002), 72–75. See also Uta Ranke Heinemann, *Eunuchs for the Kingdom of Heaven* (New York: Penguin, 1991), 211, 304. St. Jerome, as well as Pope Innocent III, though both considered early abortion a sin because it prevented the giving of life, did not consider it murder, because of the ensoulment belief within the Catholic tradition. (Fiedler and Rabben, *Rome Has Spoken.*)

14. Hans Küng, *The Catholic Church: A Short History* (New York: Random House–Modern Library, 2003), 189.

15. Karl Rahner and Herbert Vorgrimler, *Dictionary of Theology* (New York: Crossroad, 1981), 355. Richard McBrien, *Catholicism,* vol. 1 (Minneapolis: Winston Press. 1980), 164.

16. Lyons II in 1274, and Florence in 1439.

17. McBrien, *Catholicism,* 1154.

18. Hasler, *How the Pope Became Infallible,* 165.

19. Ibid. 37.

20. Fiedler and Rabben, *Rome Has Spoken,* 20.

21. Ibid., 14. See also Hasler, *How the Pope Became Infallible,* 164. Hasler's is perhaps the most detailed account of Vatican I and its struggle with the doctrine of

infallibility. He served for five years in the Vatican Secretariat for Christian Unity. It was during this time that he was given access to the Vatican Archives and discovered diaries, letters, and official documents relating to the first Vatican Council that had never been studied before.

22. Ibid., 165. The Third Council of Constantinople (668–81), the Second Council of Nicaea (787), and the Fourth Council of Constantinople (869–70)—all ecumenical Councils, the Sixth, Seventh, and Eighth consecutively.)

Notes to Chapter 4

23. John Dominic Crossan, *Jesus: A Revolutionary Biography* (New York: HarperCollins, 1995), 76–78.

24. Kenan B. Osborne, O.F.M., *Christian Sacraments in A Postmodern World: A Theology for the Third Millennium* (New York and Mahwah, N.J.: Paulist Press, 1999), 8. See also Herbert Haag, *Upstairs Downstairs: Did Jesus Want a Two-Class Church?* trans. Robert Nowell (New York: Crossroad, 1997), 11.

25. Donald Cozzens, *Faith That Dares to Speak* (Collegeville, Minn.: Liturgical Press, 2004), 11. The above citation from *Vehementer Nos* was provided also by Donald Cozzens in the same book, 9

26. There are numerous studies today dealing with this topic. I refer the reader simply to two of my own books: *Awe-Filled Wonder: The Interface of Science and Spirituality* (New York: Paulist, 2008), and *From Religion Back to Faith: A Journey of the Heart* (New York: Crossroad, 2006).

27. See Fiand, *From Religion Back to Faith,* chapter 5.

Notes to Chapter 5

28. Roger Haight, *Jesus Symbol of God* (Maryknoll, N.Y.: Orbis Books, 1999), 338.

29. See *Awe-filled Wonder* (Paulist Press), *From Religion Back to Faith, In the Stillness You Will Know, Prayer and the Quest for Healing* (all Crossroad publications)

30. John Dominic Crossan and Jonathan L. Reed, *Excavating Jesus, Beneath the Stones, Behind the Texts* (New York: HarperCollins, 2001), 300.

31. Sebastian Moore, *The Contagion of Jesus: Doing Theology as If It Mattered* (Maryknoll, N.Y.: Orbis Books, 2008), 30.

32. Ibid., 28.

33. Tad W. Guzie, S.J., *Jesus and the Eucharist* (New York: Paulist Press, 1974), 3–4 (italics added).

34. Elisabeth Schüssler Fiorenza, *In Memory of Her: A Feminist Theological Reconstruction of Christian Origins* (New York: Crossroad, 1984), 130.

35. Ibid., 57, referencing Hans Kessler (*Die Theologische Bedeutung des Todes Jesu*).

36. Herbert Haag, *Upstairs Downstairs, Did Jesus Want a Two-Class Church?* (New York: Crossroad, 1997), 81–82.

37. Ibid., 90.

38. Ibid.

39. Ibid., 93.

40. Ibid., 98.

Notes to Chapter 6

41. Walter Wink, *The Human Being: Jesus and the Enigma of the Son of Man* (Minneapolis: Fortress Press, 2001), 14.

42. Barbara Fiand, *From Religion Back to Faith: A Journey of the Heart* (New York: Crossroad, 2006), 163–64.

43. Marcus J. Borg and John Dominic Crossan, *The Last Week: What the Gospels Really Teach about Jesus's Final Days in Jerusalem* (New York: HarperCollins, 2006), 163.

44. Ibid., 29

45. Marcus J. Borg, *Jesus, Uncovering the Life, Teaching, and Relevance of a Religious Revolutionary* (New York: HarperCollins, 2006), 187.

46. Moore, *The Contagion of Jesus,* 31.

47. For an indepth and very readable study on Mark's account of that last week, see Borg and Crossan, *The Last Week.*

48. John Dominic Crossan, *Jesus: A Revolutionary Biography* (New York: Harper Collins, 1994), 153–58.

Notes to Chapter 7

49. Regis Duffy, *Real Presence: Worship, Sacraments, and Commitment* (New York: Harper & Row, 1982), 16.

50. Ibid., 24–25.

51. Ibid., 27–28.

52. Michael Himes, *Trinity*, videotape by Fischer Productions, Box 727, Jefferson Valley, NY 10535.

53. Mary T. Malone, *Women and Christianity.* vol. 2 (Maryknoll, N.Y.: Orbis Books, 2002), 204.

54. Ibid., 144.

Notes to Chapter 8

55. Martin Buber, *I and Thou* (New York: Scribners, 1958), 33–34.

56. Barbara Fiand, *From Religion Back to Faith: A Journey of the Heart* (New York: Crossroad, 2006), 157.

57. Roger Haight, *Jesus Symbol of God* (Maryknoll, N.Y.: Orbis Books, 1999), 338.

58. Cited by Aniella Jaffé, *The Myth of Meaning, Jung and the Expansion of Consciousness* (New York: Penguin Books, 1975), 34–36.

59. See His Holiness the Dalai Lama, *The Universe in a Single Atom: The Convergence of Science and Spirituality* (New York: Morgan Road Books, 2005). Also Zara Houshmand, Robert B. Livingston, and B. Alan Wallace, eds. *Consciousness at the Crossroads: Conversations with the Dalai Lama on Brain Science and Buddhism* (Ithaca, N.Y.: Snow Lion Publications, 1999).

60. For a more developed perspective of Teilhard's vision see Beatrice Bruteau, T*he Grand Option, Personal Transformation and a New Creation* (Notre Dame, Ind.: University of Notre Dame Press, 2001). Also for a shorter summary see Barbara Fiand, *From Religion Back to Faith*, 62–65.

Notes to Chapter 9

61. See Barbara Fiand, *Awe-filled Wonder: The Interface of Science and Spirituality* (New York/Mahwah, N.J.: Paulist, 2008), *From Religion Back to Faith: A Journey of the Heart; In the Stillness You Will Know, Exploring the Paths of Our Ancient Belonging; Prayer and the Quest for Healing, On Personal Healing and Cosmic Responsibility* (all New York: Crossroad, 2006, 2002, 1999 consecutively).

62. Challenging the old Euclidian claim that the whole is made up of the sum of its parts.

63. See among other sources 1215 C.E.—the Fourth Lateran Council's D806, which proclaimed: "For no similarity can be said to hold between creator and creature which does not imply a greater dissimilarity between the two."

64. Martin Heidegger, *Holzwege*, 4th ed. (Frankfurt am Main: Vittorio Klostermann, 1950), 248.

65. Barbara Fiand, *Embraced by Compassion: On Human Longing and Divine Response* (New York: Crossroad, 1993), 112-13.

66. Ralph Harper, *On Presence, Variations and Reflections* (Philadelphia: Trinity Press International, 1991), 7.

67. John V. Taylor, *The Go-Between God, The Holy Spirit and the Christian Mission* (London: SCM Press, 1972), 18.

68. "If You Have Nothing" from *The Selected Poetry of Jessica Powers*. Published by ICS Publications, Washington, D.C. All copyrights, Carmelite Monastery, Pewaukee, Wisc. Used with permission.

69. For a more detailed discussion of Eckhart's spirituality of Virgin Mothering see Barbara Fiand, *Releasement, Spirituality for Ministry* (New York: Crossroad, 1987), chapters 1 and 8.

70. Jacob Liberman, O.D., Ph.D., *Light, Medicine of the Future* (Rochester, Vt.: Bear & Company, 1991), xxii.

71. Jacques Lusseyran, *And There Was Light* (New York: Parabola Books, 1998), 19-20.

72. Fiand, *From Religion Back to Faith*, 63.

About the Author

Barbara Fiand, S.N.D., is a retired professor of philosophical and spiritual theology. She lectures and gives retreats and workshops throughout the country and abroad on issues related to holistic spirituality, prayer, the influence of quantum discoveries on spirituality, and the transformation of consciousness. Dr. Fiand is the author of nine previous books. As people are faced today with a collapsing worldview, she sees her primary work as helping them make the transition from the old and familiar to the new and at times still emerging perspectives of our time. Fiand invites us to gaze at spirituality through the context of the twenty-first century, and to use this new vision as a way to dialogue, to explore, and to take back ownership of our personal God-quest. She sees our time as an exciting opportunity for profound love and freedom.

Releasement
Spirituality for Ministry

"An important book . . . about most contemporary issues concerning ministry." —George A. Maloney, S.J.

978-0-8245-1083-1
128 pages; 5 ⅜" × 8 ¼"

Refocusing the Vision
Religious Life into the Future

The meaning of religious vows
in the context of holistic spirituality.

978-0-8245-1890-5
272 pages; 6" × 9"

In the Stillness You Will Know
Exploring the Paths of Our Ancient Belonging

978-0-8245-2650-4
176 pages; 5 ⅜" × 8 ¼"

From Religion Back to Faith
A Journey of the Heart

978-0-8245-2417-3
200 pages; 5 ⅜" × 8 ¼"

Prayer and the Quest for Healing
Our Personal Transformation and Cosmic Responsibility

978-0-8245-1812-7
192 pages; 5 ⅜"× 8 ¼"